Climb to Freedom

Seven Men Journey from the Ordinary to the Extraordinary

STEPHEN MCGHEE

DEDICATION

I dedicate this book:

To the Spirit of God, The Spirit of Aconcagua
and the Spirit that lives in each of Us.

CONTENTS

ACKNOWLEDGMENTS

First and foremost, I want to thank the Mighty Aconcagua. She is a mountain that bears the title of the tallest mountain in the world outside of Asia and towers nearly 23,000 feet. While several of the "Seven Summits" are touted as more inspiring than Aconcagua, I beg to differ. She is majestic beyond compare and offers views and vistas that are second to none in the climbing world. She, like most strong women, will decide who shares in her glory and who does not. One purpose of mine in writing this book is to share the beauty of this mountain through the written word and more fully to take those interested in joining an expedition to temper their own Aconcagua at www.AconcaguaMan.com.

Thank you, John Roger and John Morton, for teaching me about the ultimate form of freedom through the spirit. To Steve Hardison for holding me accountable to my highest form of "being". To Stephen Chandler for a dimly-lit conference room and the "flushing out" of an idea called The Aconcagua Man Project. I would like to thank Mark Graham for the interviews, conversations, and the writing. To my mother for being an author and giving me access to my own writing. To my father for the prayers. To Leslie Bartlett for the passion and for teaching me greater compassion. To my brother Doug McGhee for his example of being a man and for inspiring my next steps on the mountain. To Dave Zobl for the songs, especially the song that had us climb higher. www.Zobl.com. To Todd Musselman for the long-time friendship.

I want to thank The Aconcagua Man Team for their commitment and their excellence at collaborative leadership. To Mike Bradley for the summit and the pictures (including cover shots). To Augusto Ortega for the wisdom. To Rolo Abaca for quiet strength, Vince Ruland for his steadiness, Troy Wagner for teaching me patience, Jeff Patterson for the focus and super human commitment, Greg Aden for being gregarious and for "rock basketball," to Dennis Carruth for being our statesman and for the reality that we can all be assholes, to Eric Wiseman for getting us in manly-man shape. To Rodrigo Mujica for the challenge that got me focused. To Tom LaRotonda for his detailed orientation and his loyalty.

INTRODUCTION

I glance over my shoulder as a gust of frigid wind tries to break my stride as well as my will.

The view at 20,000 feet takes my breath away. A wall of vapor and mist, colored a burnt orange by the early morning sun, rises from the jagged, indomitable peaks of the Andes Mountains. I allow the magic of this moment to wash over me, knowing it is a sight few men will ever see.

I take a snapshot in my mind and then turn away. The summit calls to me, and I give my attention back to the narrow path that traverses a scree field of broken rocks up the face of the mighty Aconcagua: the highest mountain in the Americas.

We have been on the mountain for fourteen grueling days, hiked nearly a hundred miles, and climbed into air so rarefied that the sky and earth no longer seem like distant relatives, but rather works of art battling for our attention.

I put one step in front of another, dig my ski pole into the mountain's brittle surface, and find my rhythm again. One false step can steal a man's life, and many a man has made a false step on this treacherous stretch known as the 'windy traverse.' For nearly four hours, the Aconcagua Man Project team has battled a mix of loose sand and gravel, clawing our way up a 1,200-foot rise that has broken the spirit of hundreds of climbers over the years.

Jeff Patterson, a teammate who has been wracked with headaches and nausea during the entire climb, has fallen far behind the rest of us. Rolo, one of our Argentinean guides, shepherds Jeff up the mountain, and I can only hope that he'll reach the summit before the diminishing hours of this February day or the mountain's fickle weather makes it impossible.

We'd already lost part of our team. We'd almost been driven off the mountain by seventy-five mph winds so impressively powerful that no amount of training or preparation could steel us against the fear or the trepidation. We felt helpless, and the seven men who made up the Aconcagua team were not accustomed to feeling so powerless.

Sometimes, I had to hold on tightly. Sometimes, I had to dig deeply into a well of courage that I did not even know was there.

The weather changes on Aconcagua minute by minute, and some of those changes can be life-threatening. I knew one thing; I knew I would be a different man after this adventure: more focused, more committed, more honest.

Our American guide leads us to a cliff face that signals an end to the Canaleta, and Eric, Troy, Vince, and I pull ourselves onto a landing of ice and rock. Every bone in my body aches, and yet I'm more exhilarated than I can ever remember being.

The summit is within reach. The culmination of seven months of preparation, planning, and hard work is bearing fruit in ways I would never have imagined. I raise my head and follow a snowy traverse higher up the mountain and through a stretch of huge boulders, knowing the summit is almost within reach.

We are the first people to arrive at this point on this day, and the snow is pure and unblemished. Reaching the summit is only one part of our goal, but at this minute, it captures all of my thoughts. The summit represents the efforts of seven men coming together with a well-defined purpose. It represents growth, change, and our evolution as men.

I summon the last of my strength, and we plunge ahead.

PART I – THE PREPARATION

1 LIVING A LIFE OF INTEGRITY

This book is *about* men. It's about men who want to push themselves beyond their worlds of certainty and comfort to places of uncertainty and discovery. It's about men in search of purpose and direction beyond the boundaries that society has created for them. It's about men who have, for too long, been seeking the approval of others to justify their actions.

This is a book *for* men, but it is equally a book meant *for* women: women who see the potential for greatness in their men; women who want the men in their lives to find their passion and to pursue it with gusto and assurance; women who want to travel the path of exploration and discovery with the men in their lives and who want to celebrate their call to action.

On one level, the Aconcagua Man Project tells the story of seven men and their attempt to summit the highest peak in the Americas, Aconcagua, located in the Andes mountain range in the Argentine province of Mendoza. At 22,843 feet, it is the highest peak outside of Asia. It tells the story of their nine months of intense physical training in preparation for the climb. It tells the story of exceptional

3

commitment to a sixteen-day-climb through some of the most remote and awe-inspiring vistas in the world.

But this story goes far beyond the physicality necessary to achieve such a feat. This is a tale about a nine-month journey of working to develop physical, emotional, mental, and spiritual awareness. This is the story of seven men and their quest for integrity, inner commitment, and the truth of who they really are as men. This is a journey that explores leadership at the highest level and a commitment to the service of humanity.

Are these lofty goals? Perhaps, but these are exactly the sort of goals that every man aspires to in the depths of his heart and Soul, even if he's been told that such aspirations are too much to ask for from life. They're not.

Reaching the summit of Aconcagua serves not only as an accomplishment of the highest order, but also as a metaphor for the lives of every man and woman, for our pursuits in the business world, and for our most important relationships. Reaching the summit of this extraordinary mountain peak represents our successes, but it also represents our desire to push ourselves to find our true convictions in life and love and to dedicate ourselves to being the men and women we truly want to be.

———

Striving to be the best that we can be seems to be a lost art in society today.

———

Men in the world are becoming soft. Many of us are living lives of quiet desperation and mediocrity. Striving to conquer our "inner Aconcagua," that physiological,

4

psychological, or spiritual barrier that seems to get in the way of our true potential, no longer seems to be a priority.

Part of my role as a leadership coach and business consultant is to search for programs that are evolutionary, not just for men, but for all people; not just for my clients, but for society as a whole, and programs that touch not only the mind and the body but also the heart and the soul.

In the end, I created the Aconcagua Man Project because it served each of these exceptionally important aspects of transformation and growth. I knew the project would require a special commitment from men who wanted to achieve the extraordinary in their lives, in their businesses, and in their relationships. For me, life is too short not to seek the extraordinary. Becoming a complete, self-fulfilled man who doesn't require the approval of others is not wishful thinking. Becoming a human being devoted to the betterment of others is not a pipe dream. We were born to push our limits. Many men have just forgotten how.

Ralph Waldo Emerson once said, "Society everywhere is in conspiracy against the manhood of every one of its members. The virtue in most requests is conformity. Self-reliance is its aversion."

That quote still rings true today, maybe even more than ever. Too many of us work in jobs we don't love. Too many of us are convinced that if we put food on the table, take care of our families, and go through the motions of a normal life, we're doing exactly what we're supposed to do. Unfortunately, this doesn't account for a life filled with abundance and the gift of our deepest consciousness.

―――――

**I call it being fully committed to your
own intentions and to your own heart.
I call it living your life from a deep
and grounded purpose.**

―――――

How can we truly rear our children, to the best of our abilities, if we can't show them that living life can be pursued with vigor? How can we be of service to others in a meaningful way if we aren't being true to ourselves? The answer is: we can't.

I asked the team members of the Aconcagua Man Project to ponder an important question. What kind of man do I want to become? And I think all men should ask themselves the same question. Part of our nine-month pursuit of the Aconcagua summit—in fact, the most important part—was the search for the answer to this inquiry. I think all men have to join in this search, even if your "personal Aconcagua" involves starting a new business, getting out of a stifling relationship, losing 20 pounds., or whatever else it happens to be!

Let's speak honestly. Too many men in our society have gotten lazy. We've gotten lazy in the name of spiritual progression and personal growth. This is by no means meant to discount God and spirit. Having a meaningful relationship with God and spirit is vital, but if we've forgotten who we are and lost track of our true self, there is no way we can maximize personal growth or establish a powerful spiritual foundation. You can't have one without the other.

The Aconcagua Man Project integrates the physical with the mental and the emotional with the spiritual. The physical exercises are vigorous; the mental exercises require vigilance. We don't ignore our emotions based upon the sentiments of society, and our discussions about spirituality are robust and respectful. This is about learning and growing. And if you think about it, what else is there?

———

The Aconcagua Man Project is about recapturing our power and our courage, and this is a universal aspect of every man's "personal Aconcagua."

———

There are very few men among us who believe their lives, their businesses, and their relationships are extraordinary. Rediscovering ourselves is a matter of vigorous self-examination and hard choices. It was a huge commitment on the part of the seven men who chose to join this remarkable project, but rediscovery is a huge undertaking.

Once again, Emerson said it best. "Be brave and true to yourself. Put your heart into your work. Do these things with sincerity and you come nearer to being what you truly are: a force for good in the world."

What is he saying? He is saying that, too often, we give too much weight to the opinions of others, and we forget about the respect our own voice deserves. There is not a man alive who hasn't felt he was holding back at some point, and not one of us wants to die with that voice stifled deep inside of us. Not one of us wants to die knowing we could have inspired so many others had we only had the guts to take action.

We all want to be more integrated in our relationships. We all want to be more disciplined with our health and our well-being. We all want to learn to live in the moment and revel in the present. As I take you along on our journey up Aconcagua, my goal for you is to emerge from your own "personal Aconcagua" with complete and total clarity of who you are and how you choose to life your life. I want you to experience and appreciate the incredible nature of life again. Or, as I like to say, to suck the marrow out of life!

———

**Conquering your "personal Aconcagua"
is about regaining your mastery,
your integrity, and your vision, and acting on it.**

———

You don't need society's approval. You don't need your boss's approval or that of your spouse or best friend either. Approval comes from within. Resolve is not something some else bestows upon you. Our job, as men, is to slow down from the pressures of work and relationships enough to remember who we are. That's the only way we can really give the best to our work and our relationships. That is the only way we can truly be of service to others.

The Aconcagua Man Project is physical in the extreme. It has to be, and not simply to make the climb easier. There is, without question, a direct relationship between our physicality as men and our place in the world. Make no mistake about it. Physical strength is at the leading edge of emotional, mental, and spiritual growth.

As you navigate the pages of this book and develop a picture of your own "personal Aconcagua," committing yourself to physical fitness is a must.

Summiting five 14,000-foot peaks in Colorado's Rocky Mountains, three in the dead of winter and with full packs, is only the beginning of the Aconcagua team's nine month training schedule. Working with a high-altitude trainer for two days a week is mandatory. Each member also makes a commitment to himself and to his teammates to perform three additional days each week of personal training.

———

Accountability, responsibility, integrity, and trust: leadership begins and ends with these principles, but many men get up every morning and dismiss them.

———

How does a project like the Aconcagua Man Project restore the sense of self? It does so by creating a synergy between equally committed men who refuse to let each other off the hook, who demand accountability, and who know that an evolutionary way of Being is a goal worth every ounce of sacrifice: men who know that on the other side of sacrifice is the path to unlimited freedom.

What is transformation? Transformation is the process of creating positive changes in the physical, emotional, mental, and spiritual levels of being human. Then we can come out on the other side of any endeavor without limits, without constraints, and without excuses. Transformation gives us permission, as human beings, to answer the ultimate question: What do I want from my life?

Every man has the right to look at himself in the mirror and say, "I'm extraordinary."

Becoming extraordinary doesn't happen overnight. It requires hard work and discipline. It requires a rejection of mediocrity and the status quo.

The Aconcagua Man Project is about seven men and their quest to climb the Americas' highest peak, but it is truly much more about the men who came back down from the summit with a new view of the world, with an understanding of their dreams and the conviction to pursue them, and with a goal to make a difference in this world.

2 THE LESSONS ON JAMES PEAK

The tumultuous and near-disastrous training climb up James Peak, a glorious 13,260-foot mountain high in the Colorado Rockies, served as a microcosm example of every man's search for inner depth and purpose and how precarious that search can be.

I like to describe the Aconcagua Man Project as an exploration of life and leadership, as applied to the lives of seven men for the betterment of humanity. The more clarity we have at the "self" level helps translate into more clarity at the "service" level, and that was a commitment we had all made to each other: to come down from Aconcagua and our nine-month journey dedicated to making a real difference in society.

Martin Luther King is one of the finest examples of this. He knew himself as well as any man can. Had he not, I have to wonder if he could have so completely dedicated himself to his movement of equality. I believe he could not have done so.

November 20, 2010.

Greg Aden called me at ten in the morning, exactly two hours before our team was scheduled to begin our ascent of James Peak, and his call proved to be a harbinger of a very dicey and somewhat discombobulated training exercise.

Greg couldn't make it. I could hear the stress in his voice. I didn't know the cause, but I knew that he and his wife Laura were in the process of adopting a baby boy from Russia. She was also pregnant with their first child: her second. A highly successful entrepreneur with two flourishing businesses, it wasn't as if Greg didn't already have enough going on in his life. But in addition to all that, he had made a serious commitment to the men of the Aconcagua Man Project.

We didn't miss training sessions—that was part of the commitment—and this overnight trek was one high-altitude climb that we all considered to be key to the preparation for our January ascent of a mountain far higher and more punishing than James Peak.

"I can't make the climb," he said, and I could sense how overwhelmed he was.

He went on to explain his reasons—all good, sound, and logical reasons—which prompted me to ask, "Greg, do you want me to be your friend or your coach?"

His answer surprised me. "I want you to be both."

I said, "Listen, Greg, the friend in me understands that you're in a situation, and you want an 'out.' But the coach in me sees this differently. You've got a tremendous amount of things going on, and this isn't the first time you've had to cancel on a commitment. I want you to promise yourself that you'll take some time to put all the things you have going on into perspective and make sure you're not rationalizing your choices to yourself or to others in your life."

This wasn't just a leadership lesson for Greg. If anything, Greg errs on the side of trying to do too many things to the best of his ability. How many of us have over committed ourselves? What is the result of that in our lives and business? One thing you can be certain of is that it does not work long-term. It creates an endemic problem in terms of not allowing our deepest integrity to emerge. For this reason, I feel the most powerful word in the English language for someone like Greg is NO. To say NO to things that are not of the absolutely deepest import.

As it was, minus our one team member, we met at the trailhead at noon, facing a snow-packed trail, winds in excess of 50 mph, ground blizzards, and whiteout conditions. This was a chance for our team to test its cold-weather gear: shoes, outwear, tents, sleeping bags, and new backpacks, which were all items of extraordinary importance for Aconcagua, where fifty degrees below zero wind chills and 75 mph winds are a very real possibility.

———

**It was here at the trailhead,
that we faced a second obstacle.**

———

We hadn't done an adequate job of organizing who would carry what and how, so now we were using invaluable climbing time doing what we should have done earlier instead. It seemed to take us forever, as a team, to get on the trail. Another lesson learned.

The turmoil continued when I realized my double-mountaineering boots didn't fit the snowshoes we had outfitted ourselves with. I had just committed one of the cardinal sins of high altitude climbing: a lack of preparation. On a broader scale, I had committed a cardinal sin for any endeavor, be it professional or personal, but especially one with an unknown outcome.

Were something like this to happen on Aconcagua, trying to trek through snow and ice to a base camp at 18,000 feet, my dream of summiting would be dashed. I could forget it: nine months of training would be down the drain. Here I was the organizer of this remarkable project, a leadership coach and team leader—breaking one of my most basic rules: prepare, and then prepare some more.

However, there was an upside to this inauspicious beginning. Our high-altitude trainer, twenty-eight-year-old Eric Wiseman, had insisted we test our new gear in a setting not unlike what we might see on Aconcagua. This was our chance; it was better to make mistakes here, where the mistakes could be rectified, than at 18,000 feet where the only option might be turning back.

We set out, slightly behind schedule, but determined. The climb was excruciating. The weather was bone-chilling. A sense of adventure was tempered by a tiny voice in the back of my head asking, "Why in the hell are we doing this? I could be at home watching the NFL playoffs and sitting in front of a warm fire."

**The uncertainty cannot be overstated,
but the uncertainty was part of the attraction;
this was the barrier we had committed
ourselves to breaking through.**

We had a goal: to summit the highest mountain in the world outside of Asia. That was sufficient motivation to get us up James Peak. But that wasn't all there was to it. We had also made a commitment to the rest of our team, and letting the team down was not an option.

You can achieve the extraordinary by doing the ordinary. And in this case, it was putting one foot in front of the other, hour after hour, until we reached our base camp.

I paid the price for my lack of diligence and preparation. I was forced to post-hole with a fifty-pound pack to our base camp, which took three-and-a-half hours and those were some of the most exhausting and excruciating miles of my life. I am a strong athlete. Our team was filled with experienced guys. And yet here was another lesson that I would bring down from James Peak as a result of this weekend: experience is a wonderful asset, but not if it leads to being cocky.

We set up camp in three feet of snow and with temperatures well below freezing; with cold weather tents and sleeping bags tested to twenty five degrees below zero, huddling together over hot tea and freeze-dried food. In the midst of melting snow and checking fuel supplies, we planned our ascent. And during all of that, there was a sense of adventure matched only by the power of the

15

moment. We were staring at a sky so filled with stars that you could think, "That is the most beautiful sky I have ever seen." The next day, we set out for the summit in high winds and whiteout conditions: very intimidating.

Rule number one on the mountain: take care of yourself first, so that you can then take care of your team. This is true in leadership as well. It may not be obvious to some people reading this book. But think about it. If you are not well-prepared yourself, how can you ever lead another?

I believe in collaborative leadership. Yes, there are times when one person steps to the forefront and others defer to that person—for this project, Eric was our trainer, and I was the project's organizer—but this does not relieve any of us, either on the mountain or in our personal or professional lives, not to think for ourselves, to take responsibility, and to be accountable.

We were about to test this theory.

We left our camp early on that Sunday morning, looking into the darkening sky. If the day before was any barometer, I knew a summit to the top of this formidable peak, given the conditions, could be an "iffy" proposition. In retrospect, I should have listened more closely to my own inner leader, but I was with a group of tenacious, determined men and turning back was not a part of their default thinking.

We were joined for this assault by Lisa Sleeth and Vince Ruland, who were making the trek on skis and without the burden of fifty-pound-packs. Vince, an extremely experienced mountaineer, was the newest member of our team. He and I had only just recently become acquainted, and this was the first time he'd met any of the other members of our group. This added another dynamic. How would Vince fit in? How would the team respond? It was an awkward morning, and I continued to deny the obvious. We were heading into a nightmare of a storm.

———

We set out. It was tough going; five hours of hard climbing through two- and three-foot-drifts with fifty pounds on our backs.

———

The higher we climbed, the more apparent it was that we were facing a whiteout on the summit. A whiteout is exactly what it sounds like: snow coming down so thickly and winds so vicious that visibility is essentially non-existent.

By the time we reached the summit, the freezing weather and raging wind contributed to the confusion that would cause us to get separated. Visibility was no more than twenty feet, and probably less.

This was no place to stop and warm ourselves or to eat a protein bar. The winds were stinging my face, and Lisa was moving into a hypothermic situation. We had to get off that mountain, and there was not time to celebrate our summit. Vince and Lisa skied down the summit snowfall, and Eric and Dennis, the youngest and oldest members of the Aconcagua team, both extremely fit, followed. In the confusion, Troy, Jeff, and I slipped off the "back side" of the mountain. Our visibility was essentially zero, and we failed to consult a compass to double-check our trajectory; a huge mistake. We missed our mark by no more than ten feet in a given direction and headed down the west side of the peak.

We descended seven hundred feet before the realization that we were lost settled deep in the pit of my stomach. Nothing looked familiar. Our teammates were nowhere to be seen. I turned to Jeff and saw the fatigue on his face. Troy was outwardly calm, but there was no mistaking the concern of our sudden predicament.

"We're lost, guys. We fucked up," I said.

My mind was occupied checking off things like our water and food supplies when it dawned on me to check my cell phone reception. Remarkably, there was a signal at 13,000 feet and hours away from the nearest city. I dialed Vince's number, praying he would answer, and he did. I could hear the alarm in his voice as I described our situation, and the last words out of his mouth were, "You're in a really dangerous situation. You have to turn around and climb back to the summit. Right now."

Vince described it this way.

> Eric and Dennis stood halfway down the summit ridge, looking back up toward the top. The extreme upper part of the mountain was completely shrouded by howling winds and blowing snow, but we should have been able to see the rest of the team descending. We couldn't. It was clear that something was very wrong.
>
> From where Lisa and I were waiting, we saw Dennis and Eric drop their packs and head back toward the summit. What a sight to see; Dennis, at sixty-seven years young, heading back up into the teeth of that storm out of concern for his friends and teammates.
>
> I, myself, climbed to a nearby high point: a lookout that afforded me a view of the northeast side

of the mountain, and my stomach jumped into my mouth. That sheer and ominous side of James Peak plunged a thousand feet straight down, and three guys with fifty-pound packs on their backs would have little or no chance of surviving the drop.

When I saw Eric and Dennis reappear a moment later, descending from the summit without the rest of the team, I knew we probably needed to call in Search and Rescue. Lisa and I skied toward the descending pair, and Eric informed us that he and Dennis had found tracks heading down the west side of the Mountain.

I was thinking that at least the terrain on the west side represented safer terrain when my cell phone rang. I couldn't believe it. It was Stephen calling, and his voice sounded pretty darn calm.
"We're lost," he said.

"Give me your GPS coordinates." When I put the coordinates alongside the information that Eric had armed us with, I knew that there was only one way to get things straightened out. The lost party had to make an about-face, retrace their steps to the summit, and get back to the right side of the mountain.

At this point, Eric, Dennis, Vince, and Lisa had no way of knowing that Troy, Jeff, and I had descended seven hundred vertical feet and that we would need more than an hour and fifteen minutes to find our way back to the summit. With the temperature plummeting and the wind and snow gaining strength, the foursome turned their attention to alerting Search and Rescue while the three of us post-holed our way back toward the mountain's inhospitable summit.

Despite the verbal communication that we had just exchanged minutes before, they had no way of really knowing our true location. I would find out later that Vince used his phone again and dialed 911 for the first time in his life. It had to be a surreal feeling to be explaining to the dispatcher that they had three team members lost in a whiteout near the summit of James Peak.

Vince's next thirty minutes were spent in conversation with the county's Search and Rescue and the local Sheriff's office, and every attempt to reach me again on my cell phone failed.

By this time, there was nothing else that Lisa, Vince, Eric, or Dennis could do for us, given the extreme conditions, except to insure their own safety, so they decided to descend to a more protected vantage point, hoping and praying that we had received their message and understood Vince's directive.

———

We don't always stop to consider how our actions affect other people, and it wouldn't dawn on me until later just how much stress and anxiety our poor decision-making had caused our comrades.

———

Facing their own battle with frostbite and increasingly precarious conditions, Lisa and Vince turned on their skis, and Eric and Dennis shouldered their packs. But they hadn't gone more than a hundred yards when they heard shouting.

Vince would later write:

I turned and looked up the mountain. I was thrilled to see one, and then two, and finally all three climbers appear at the summit! The guys had self-rescued!

And indeed we did self-rescue, but not without a huge risk. All three of us were completely exhausted, dehydrated, and clearly shaken by the prospect of stepping off the 1000-foot crevasse that the west side of James Peak is noted for.

This was a situation that could easily have gone south, but it didn't. Everyone came together as a team, and our mutual actions prevented a catastrophe. Our training as a team worked. We stayed calm, accessed our situation, and communicated. No one panicked, and I was proud to see that the trust level we'd developed with one another over the last six months not only survived a crisis situation, but also proved to be one of our greatest assets.

————

When I talk about leadership, the discussion has to center around four traits: awareness, integrity, accountability, and trust.
And it is trust that inevitably ties the four together.

————

In this situation, there was no finger pointing. No one played the "blame game." In fact, the most prevalent emotion of all was gratitude. We'd all survived more or less unscathed. This was an opportunity to learn. I wanted to make sure we took advantage of it.

We assembled again at our base camp, and the processing began almost immediately. Lesson one: Awareness. Be "present" and ready for every contingency. Lesson two: Integrity. Listen to your gut and speak up if you know you are heading into a storm or going in the wrong direction. Lesson three: Accountability. Be responsible for yourself and own your part in any situation with the potential of going south. Lesson Four: Trust. Trust yourself and your team. Stay calm and take solution-oriented steps without escalating unnecessary emotions.

The conditions on the summit were as bad as they could get, and the splintering of the team was inexcusable. The communication breakdown that we suffered could not happen on the slopes of Aconcagua. It was as simple as that. No one on the team disagreed with that assessment, and we committed ourselves to making certain it never happened again, even on a training climb.

———

In the end, we emerged stronger and smarter as individuals and more cohesive and committed as a team.

———

We also gained a seventh teammate when Vince decided to join us, in spite of what had happened on James Peak, because of how we had all performed in the face of a crisis situation.

In my book *Learning to Believe the Unbelievable*, I talk extensively about the miracle of discomfort. This is the inevitable outcome of stepping outside the box and

22

embracing your edge. Do that and you're going to feel uncomfortable. That is the inevitable outcome of recognizing your limitations as illusions, because that's all they are. The limitations we've created for ourselves very often seem real because that's all we know. But the absolute truth is that the minute you make yourself uncomfortable is the minute you begin to grow and change as a person. That's a miracle in and of itself.

Most of us don't take the time to really get to know ourselves; in fact, many of us don't really know ourselves at all. We are robots of society. We live and act based upon the dictates of society, as opposed to living life on our own terms. Getting into the hard work of really knowing ourselves is, frankly, inconvenient for most of us. It takes work. We like quick fixes. We like things to be easy.

How many of us really know ourselves? Furthermore, how many of us take the time to find out more about who we really are? It's considered by many to be a waste of time to reflect upon one's life. Is it? Well, it's not according to the Aconcagua Man Project.

3 FROM IDEA TO REALITY

The Aconcagua Man Project began as an idea early in 2010. I flew to Phoenix, AZ, to meet with my friend and Master Coach, Steve Chandler, to flush out the specifics of this unreasonable venture. Chandler assisted me in putting rocket fuel on the whole idea. You can learn about Steve's great work at www.SteveChandler.com

I issued invitations to well over one hundred men, and I admit that the entry-level requirements were considerable. I was not looking for guys who just wanted to conquer a mountain. Anyone can join an excursion up Aconcagua if he or she has the wherewithal and the time.

This project began with a clear understanding that awareness, integrity, accountability, and trust were four necessary elements. The project began with an absolute focus on awareness and learning. From day one, we would be challenging ourselves every step of the way to become more attentive of our physical, emotional, mental, and spiritual selves.

We would be exploring, at a very high level, what it means to be a true leader. This was not necessarily the person with the highest position or the greatest authority.

Not at all! True leaders are people with unabridged enthusiasm for their own lives and their own existence, and, without question, the inner drive to be a part of an experience and a world far greater than themselves. True leaders are creating miracles big and small every single day. They inspire others to do the same. They exemplify the call to action that is the foundation for real leadership.

These are key elements in my repertoire as a leadership consultant and business coach. I believe with every fiber of my being that melding caring and leadership into one effective working model is the key to creating results, and I wanted my team members to understand my commitment to this ideal. Part of my job would be to assist this team in becoming a collaboration of top-flight leaders, as opposed to the classic model that is cast around one leader and his or her band of willing followers. As part of our agreement, each of us would also agree to impart our knowledge of the world on the rest of the team.

———

I wanted men on my team who wanted to play their edge and craved a vehicle to explore new horizons.

———

I wanted men on my team who saw leadership as an ever-evolving process made manifest by a willingness to learn. I wanted men on my team who were open to the concept of collaborative leadership as a means of producing a common result. I wanted men on my team who could envision serving others and who saw service to the idea of a better world as a worthy endeavor.

The "Invitation Only" brochure and audio CD issued to this selective group came right to the point. It said:

The Aconcagua Man Project is a nine-month program created for seven unique men who are willing to push themselves to the edge of their physical, emotional, mental, and spiritual boundaries...Imagine yourself standing at the summit of Aconcagua with the strength of a mountain as your internal fortitude. Your life will never be the same again...You will stop seeking approval and claim the clarity and integration of your life...This is your chance to turn what is ordinary in your life into the extraordinary. You will leave this program as a more deliberate and integrated man.

The responses I received were enlightening and very relevant to our discussions in this book. A large number of men said, "I want to do it. I know how important this could be. I know how much value I would get out of it. I know I would return from such a commitment a changed person. I want to do it. But I can't."

And what were their biggest obstacles? Time and money, just as with so many of the things that we "want to do, but can't."

Yes, time and money are real necessities. But here's the thing. In truth, it's really not about time and money. You and I know that if we want something badly enough and truly understand its value, we can find the time and money. By and large, time and money are excuses not to take action. A lack of money might be a burden. Finding free time can be a struggle. No doubt about it. But neither one is a legitimate reason for not doing something, if your life is devoted to being a leader. When we talk about the reasons we give for choosing not do something, they are almost always actually steeped in complacency and fear.

I certainly did receive an array of legitimate reasons for not participating. One man had already planned a trip to Italy to celebrate his daughter's graduation from college. Okay, that one I understood. But each of us—you, me, the man on the street—inherently seeks those defining moments that signify our thirst for a more meaningful life. Yes, it could be a healthier lifestyle. It could be the pursuit of a new career. It could be a commitment to community service. I have my list. You have your list. And if you don't have your list, then making that list can be a defining moment in its own right.

I interviewed dozens of men. A team began to take shape.

Eric Wiseman

It began with our high altitude trainer, Eric Wiseman, who is twenty-eight. With a finance degree from DePaul University in Chicago, Eric became an investment banker who saw no future working in a cubicle ten hours a day. So when he had the chance to move back to his home state of Colorado, he didn't hesitate. He'd grown up hiking and camping with his family along Grand Junction's western slope, and the mountains were calling to him again.

He met his wife Adina while he was waiting tables and dreaming of a career as a mountain guide. With her encouragement, he took the plunge in early 2010, drawing up plans for his company, 14er Fitness. His first informal gig was at his wife's company retreat in beautiful Steamboat Springs, Colorado, where Eric was charged with organizing a hike to Fish Creek Falls. His group of ten grew to a company of twelve when an overweight and (by their own admission) out-of-shape couple asked if they could join the excursion. Eric said yes, of course, though he knew they might be in for some trouble along the way.

Eric stayed with that couple throughout most of the hike, encouraging them every step of the way, and when they reached the furthermost of Fish Creek's falls, they had tears of joy in their eyes.

When Eric saw this, he knew he had found his calling. He saw how a physical commitment could also fuel a desire to push mental, emotional, and spiritual boundaries, and he was exactly the type of team member I was seeking.

Fate brought Eric and me together when he and his wife worked with my brother Doug on the purchase of some horse property in the mountain town of Evergreen. Eric was still searching for some direction for his new company when he and I first began talking. When I asked him point-blank what it was that he really wanted to do, he verbalized, for the first time, his desire to create a program culminating in the Grand Canyon's famous Rim-to-Rim hike.

Then he set out to make it happen.

When I heard the approach Eric intended to take to train for his Grand Canyon group—a regimen that included two training sessions a week, plus weekend hikes to elevation—I realized his vision was similar to the one I had for my Aconcagua team: a vigorous training program for nine months, culminating in seven men who were in prime condition to challenge the highest peak in the world outside of Asia.

His assigned job for the Aconcagua Man Project, beginning back in June, was to flesh out plans for regular training cycles to places like Red Rocks amphitheater and

29

Lookout Mountain, along with a series of 14,000-foot hikes to places like Grizzly Peak and Long's Peak.

I knew that Eric would be training a bunch of guys somewhat senior to him in age and, in many ways, far more experienced. But I saw a young man who was up to the challenge. I saw his focus. I saw his determination. He was as likable as a person could be. He had a steady, unwavering gaze and an exceptional smile. But I also saw a guy who would hold the men in his charge accountable. He would push them, encourage them, and keep them on task. And he would never let them forget what they were working for: the summit of both their inner Aconcagua and the mountain of the same name.

Eric got it; he knew that the two were related. And I knew I'd found an exceptional team member.

Dennis Carruth

From the youngest member of our team to the oldest, I met Dennis Carruth, who is sixty-seven-years-young as we like to say, through his wife Penney. Penney is a valued client and a great friend of mine who is at the top of the real estate profession in Aspen. I mentioned the Aconcagua project to her, and she introduced her husband to the idea.

Your first thought when you meet Dennis is that you hope to be as fit as he is when you're sixty-seven. Your second thought is that you hope to have the same vitality for living when you're his age.

Dennis has three passions: skiing, entrepreneurship, and family, not necessarily in that order. He was made for the outdoors, spending every spare minute of his early years on his aunt's ranch in Steamboat Springs and developing into a world-class ski racer. By the time Dennis graduated from high school, he had won dozens of A-Class races, skied alongside such skiing greats as Billy Kidd and Bud Werner, and made the North American Ski Team. Not bad for a kid who couldn't have weighed more than 155 pounds soaking wet.

He won a scholarship to the University of Wyoming, chose business over engineering, and earned his MBA. He figured he was headed for corporate America until a stint with MCA Financial in Denver sparked an inherent love for entrepreneurship. I remember one of our first conversations, when he explained it as well as anyone possibly could, saying, "Entrepreneurship gives the people of this great country the ability to work hard, to open doors of opportunity, to make something of themselves, and to create something of value for others. And just maybe they can make some money in the process."

I look at that statement and it all fits. By the time Dennis was thirty-five, he was the president of a real estate company called the Ken Caryl Development Group. Six years later, he formed his own company, Village Homes, and he never looked back. Of course, he's pragmatic enough to call real estate development, "The greatest form of delayed gratification there is."

This is a quote Dennis likes to share with his three grown children, Allison, Ryan, and Ashley, but the one he's far more adamant about is this, "Find your passion, whatever it is. Find it, pursue it, and make it a part of your life."

He and I talked early on about making a mark in the world, and his perspective could not be more valid: making a difference is about doing things that are of value to others; it's about pushing the envelope of knowledge and creativity; it's about gaining the respect of family, friends, and peers.

By the time that Dennis and I met last spring, his business, like every other real estate developer's in Colorado, if not in the entire country, had taken its lumps in the face of the recent housing and banking crisis. He was seeking the kind of transformation that ski racing had given him in his teens and early twenties and that fatherhood had given him in his thirties and forties.

Dedicating nine months of his life to the exploration of his "inner Aconcagua" while training for an ascent of the great mountain itself, especially at a time when his business was on shaky ground, may have seemed overly adventurous to some. But it didn't seem like that to his friends or his kids, and especially not to his wife. The message was clear: You have to go for it.

Dennis had a vision: transformation, service, and the search for purpose. So he made the leap. He said yes to the Aconcagua Man Project.

Our team was expanding.

Greg Aden

Greg and I were roommates at Fort Lewis College in Durango. You will never find a more beautiful setting for two guys who loved the outdoors, loved to play, and thrived on competition. Greg was the lean guy who was always on the go and always pushing the envelope. It was no surprise that he pursued a degree in Business Administration, with a focus on sales and marketing, given the success he has had in the business world since. But business—and the business of getting an education—were only two of his interests. He also pursued his love of the theater and developed a citywide sports show broadcast by the college's own radio station. Greg could interview coaches and players as comfortably as he could do the play-by-play for a high school football game.

Greg's first question when it comes to life and business has always been, "Why not?" Why not push the envelope? Why not try something new? Why not take a chance? He has never believed in taking the easy way out. He has never believed in the age-old excuse for inactivity that so many of us use every day: I'm too busy. In Greg's view of the world, suggesting that you're too busy is just another way of saying it's not important to you. That's fine, but why not just say so? But if it is important to you, then not taking action is inexcusable.

Greg was one of the first people I ever met who I could truly call a "seeker of truth." That's all he asks of other people: just the truth. No excuses or equivocations. Just speak the truth and move on.

Greg has been working in the hotel business in some capacity since the day he left college for a position with the Tamarron Resort just outside of Durango. It was there that he met his first mentor, a gentleman named Ken Dodd, and first heard the quote: "You don't know when you're going to meet someone who's going to change your life." And that's one thing I know about Greg: he is one of those people.

Greg took to the marketing world like a fish to water and became one of Marriott's top producers, selling conferences to meeting planners. After saying no to a lucrative offer from Disney, Greg left Marriott for a new career with a financial services company in Texas. This lasted until 1997, when he found his niche selling hotel franchises for Holiday Inn Worldwide. The company became InterContinental Hotels Group, representing seven hotels in all, and Greg has been their number one producer in Texas for the last thirteen years.

By the time Greg and I began discussing the Aconcagua Man Project and the prospect of scaling the highest peak in the world outside of Asia, his life was already in a state of incredible transition.

He was newly married as of March 20, 2010. He, his new wife Laura, and Laura's daughter had taken up residence in Denver, which meant significant travel time back and forth from Texas. He and Laura were also talking about expanding their family, and part of this discussion centered on the possibility of adopting a child from Russia. And after thirteen years with his current company, Greg was exploring several new career options.

He was fit, but he wanted to give more focus to his physical, psychological, and spiritual health. For someone whose business endeavors had always allowed him a certain level of autonomy, he wanted the challenge of working with a team of equally motivated men. He also saw the Aconcagua Man Project as a way of putting his money where his mouth was, so to speak, in giving back to the community and inspiring others to do the same.

After signing on as the fourth member of my team, Greg wrote this:

> *As I really look into what the Aconcagua Man Project is all about and why I personally joined it, the following questions jump out. Where are my limits? What can I achieve personally, physically, spiritually, and emotionally, if I truly apply all my learning AND train myself to listen to a higher calling? What/where is my true potential relative to service and inspiration to others?*

Let the training begin!

Troy Wagner

Troy is one of the most humble men I've ever met, which is one of the reasons he became the fifth member of our team last year.

Troy is a thirty-eight-year-old software engineer and business operations officer for Level 3 Communications in Denver. I begin with that because it was Troy's desire to find more meaning in his life that first brought us together. It's not that Troy doesn't find his work fulfilling or challenging; Troy has the kind of mindset that is always exploring, always learning, and always dissecting. His work at Level 3 provides that. What Troy was searching for, when we first met, was more passion in his life and a true sense of purpose. There had to be something for him beyond the challenges of the workplace, and Troy was looking for a vehicle.

I was introduced to Troy nearly three years ago by his now ex-wife Jennifer. Jennifer was wise enough back then to see that Troy wasn't satisfied either at home or at work, and she suggested Troy sit in on a few coaching sessions with me.

What Troy and I discovered—and this was one of his first demonstrations of speaking the truth without equivocation—was that he had spent most of his life seeking the approval of everyone, from his parents and his wife to his colleagues at work and his teammates on the football field.

Troy is a Colorado native, born and raised there. While all of his friends were watching football on the weekends, Troy was scratching an itch that still gets him up to the mountains these days: skiing. Skiing and freedom went hand in hand.

He skied, he played tennis, he swam, and he practiced Tae Kwon Do. He discovered a love for individual sports because it allowed him to dissect every move, every technique, and every nuance. Picking things apart allowed him to put them back together in the most proficient way.

His interest in traveling to the Mendoza Province of Argentina to climb Aconcagua was rooted as much in his interest of culture and ethnicity as it was in summiting the actual mountain itself. This cultural fascination began when he was only thirteen and was traveling regularly to South America where his stepfather was working in the gold business.

Troy took it further. He began studying Spanish. He fell in love with Venezuela and her people. His pursuit of a second language led him to a three-month adventure in Costa Rica.

Back in the states, Troy's thirst for learning led him to study mechanical engineering and international management at the University of Denver: as some might see it, an odd combination. He saw it as a way of bridging the gap between the people who want to make money and the people who help them make money.

When the work world called, Troy set his sights on the IT industry and found a job with MCI doing software testing. The experience led him to a year-long-contract in Kentucky before the allure of the Rockies brought him back to Denver and a position with Level 3.

Unfortunately, five years of a less-than-satisfying marriage led to his divorce last May. By then, Troy was a man asking the most pertinent of all questions: What do I really want out of life? He was searching. He was asking the question, but the answer was still illusive.

Troy was one of the men I sent my Aconcagua invitation to. It resonated with him. He was single again. He was invested enough in his company that the month leave he would have to take in January 2011 was not out of the question.

He wanted to get in shape again. He wanted to rediscover his love for the outdoors. He had spent the last five years creating excuses for being inactive. He'd shunned his love of skiing. It was time for Troy to do something for Troy, and this was it.

He called me up and said, "I'm in," and I had team member number five.

Jeff Patterson

I met Jeff in my first year at the University of Santa Monica. We were both studying for a Masters in Spiritual Psychology. I liked him immediately.

He is a professional life coach who shares an extraordinary connection with nature. When I introduced him to the idea of the Aconcagua project, he was a long way from his Los Angeles roots and was living in the mountain community of Glenwood Springs, Colorado.

Jeff has an impressive mantra that made him a perfect candidate for the climb. He calls it, *"Living with the end in mind."*

He says, "When you live with the end in mind, you are actually programming your mind for success and setting in motion a powerful chain of events. Everything we see in our lives starts in our minds."

Jeff's consulting company is called Seed Coaching. His approach is unique. He seeks out clients who want to

37

experience, at the highest level, the presence of Spirit in their everyday lives. This begins with a premise that makes Jeff the perfect Aconcagua team member, and that premise is a fundamental understanding that each person's nature is divine. What an exceptional, compelling thought that is. And Jeff believes that any issue in our lives results from a misunderstanding of this core truth that we are wholly and completely special.

The word "SEED" in Seed Coaching is an acronym for Seeing, Experiencing, and Expressing the Divinity that lives within each of us. How extraordinary is this view of life? You can read more about Jeff's inspiring perspectives on his website, www.RadicallyAliveNow.com.

For Jeff, the idea of scaling the great Aconcagua, juxtaposed against the idea of scaling an even greater "inner Aconcagua," was too appealing to pass up. But what appealed to him even more was the journey we intended to take in preparing ourselves for it physically, emotionally, mentally, and spiritually over a nine-month-period.

While preparing for this journey, Jeff and I talked in length about the extraordinary value of "living with the end in mind." It comes down to this: the more energy you give to a successful outcome, the more you believe it will happen. Your body and spirit begin to react in a positive way to this positive mental stimulus of moving forward and taking action.

Jeff is in his late thirties, and he made it clear to me that there was no value for him in seeking the summit of Aconcagua, if that was the only goal our team had. But, of course, he knew me well enough to know that the project was a lot bigger than that. Happiness doesn't automatically become a reality just because we realize a goal. That thing we call happiness—or the things that truly manifest happiness, like love and joy and peace and harmony—are all right there inside of us.

For me, it was one of those small miracles that we've been talking about, when a project of this magnitude could entice the likes of Jeff to join us.

There would be some fearful moments in our journey to the summit of Aconcagua, and there would also be some fearful moments in the revealing of our true nature during those nine months.

The fear was inevitable, but at least Jeff and I were coming at it with a similar mind-set. It was not about trying to get rid of the fear. That wasn't it at all. Success is not determined by the depth or the severity of the fear we're feeling, but by how we respond to the fear.

Vince Ruland

An adventure wouldn't be an adventure if there wasn't a little intrigue to spice things up, and our team got a dose of that when my former wife Sally introduced me to the new man in her life, Vince Ruland. It was all with the best interest of the Aconcagua Man Project in mind, since Vince was a longtime mountaineer, and Sally saw him as a prospective addition to our team.

If you look in the dictionary, a mountaineer is defined as someone who climbs mountains for sport. Not so fast.

Vince does, in fact, refer to himself as a mountaineer, but his definition is a little different. "A mountaineer is someone who is versed in an extensive repertoire of climbs, from the most technical to the most labor intensive, who has mastered a variety of climbing techniques, and who understands and appreciates the equipment needed in any given situation."

Vince exemplifies that description. His love affair with climbing and "God's creations" began when he was twelve and had an opportunity to summit the Middle Sister near Bend, Oregon, his hometown. In retrospect, he told me, the event was life-changing and transformational.

When he was fourteen, he and his fellow Explorer Scouts were invited to join the Lane County Search and Rescue unit, and excursions carried out in old Army jeeps with even older Army cots for overnight affairs had him snow-camping in the Cascade Mountains, trekking in the high deserts, and exploring the likes of Cape Perpetua on the rugged Oregon coast.

The mountains in particular became his personal church. He calls them "one of the few places where you can be fully present."

Vince has done hundreds of solo climbs, climbing most of Colorado's 14ers with only his dog at his side, but he discovered an appreciation for the team climb in 1999, when he joined a group of twelve who were doing a four-day summit of Mount Rainer in Washington state.

Climbing, he told me when we first met, is not just about reaching the summit of a mountain. You have to be comfortable with the process, and you have to be inspired by the journey. And you have to be committed to the goals that loom out on the horizon; goals that drive you beyond any individual hike. That's why you commit to getting up in the morning for that jog in the snow or that hour on the treadmill; because you know there's another mountain out there waiting to kick your ass.

This isn't just a lesson about climbing a physical mountain; this is a metaphor for our daily lives, our relationships, and our forays into the business world. You have to stay on top of your game; you have to keep challenges out in front of you. Otherwise, as a human being, you will live out a life of quiet desperation.

Vince is a program manager for Raytheon. He and his team of fifty people build systems meant to fly earth-observing satellites for the National Aeronautics and Space Administration and the National Oceanic and Atmospheric Administration. He's responsible for managing a budget of hundreds of millions of dollars and some of the most sensitive equipment around. It keeps him busy.

When I first met Vince, his Raytheon team was planning for a major launch in October. He was also going through a divorce. He was dealing with the difficult task of preparing his two daughters, Mekala and Gianna, for living their lives under two different roofs. Trekking one of the planet's seven summits may have been a lifelong goal, but the timing could hardly have been worse. He had never taken three weeks off in his life, least of all with a new project looming on the horizon and the financial and personal obstacles staring him in the face at the time.

Then Sally challenged him with one of those incredibly hard-hitting questions that too many of us often evade. "How will you feel in five years if you turn down this opportunity, a dream you've had since you were twelve?"

That hit Vince hard. How often had he advised his own daughters to chase their dreams.

And so he did. On a chilly night in November, after a brutal training regimen at Red Rocks Amphitheater, he committed to the Aconcagua Man Project. He validated our team's commitment; not only to the climb, but to the ideals we had all set for the project. He committed himself not only to being in the best possible physical condition, but also to being a valued and contributing team member.

We had our seventh team member.

———

It was time to prepare.
It was time to start moving from the vision
to the actual nuts and bolts of
making the vision a reality.

———

Actually, this preparation began long before Vince joined the team, and I was doing my research even before the six original members were on board. The fact is you can't always have all your ducks in order before you make the leap into something new. If you did, you might never act.

I wanted a climbing guide service with an exceptional success rate on Aconcagua and I found one based in Mendoza, Argentina. The company was called Aventuras Patagonicas and they boasted twenty-eight years' worth of guiding experience for every major mountain in the world. So in June, I sat down with their director, Rodrigo Mujica, whose own experience included twenty-eight expeditions to Aconcagua. Who better to talk to!

"You won't do it," Rodrigo said when I told him of my plans for the project. He wasn't being openly critical. He had apparently heard enough of these "hair-brained" schemes to know that an exclusive team-type project like ours rarely worked. I didn't take it as an insult, but I did take it as a challenge.

I said to him that he really did not know what I could and could not do, and that if I said I was going to bring seven men to climb the mountain, I would. The truth is that I did not have even one member of our team in place when I met Rodrigo.

"What type of a down payment would you need to secure a spot for us in January of next year?" I asked. He told me, and I wrote the check.

"Okay. I like that you have an ego, because it takes big confidence to climb a High Peak," he said, nodding his head and agreeing to my terms: seven men, three guides, full accommodations, and a window of three-plus weeks. We shook hands. "You have a deal."

This was a huge step.

I wanted the commitment. I wanted to have something on the line that signified I was all in. This also provided me with the kind of hard and fast information that I could share with the team. We had a guiding service, and they were one of the very best in the business. Now it was up to us to be ready.

January 16, 2011 may have seemed a long way off then, but it really wasn't.

4 CLIMB TO FREEDOM

What happens?

As young people, we have dreams. Some of them may seem crazy, such as becoming a great business tycoon or running for President. You get my meaning. Are they far-fetched? Maybe. Are they silly? No, I think they are inspired.

Some of them are more pragmatic, such as starting your own online business or publishing your own book. Do they require work? Of course they do. Are they achievable? Definitely.

Maybe we put off pursuing some of these dreams, either crazy or pragmatic, because the "should" in life distracts us. We should go to school; a college education, we've all been told, is a necessity. Maybe we've been told that college is not an experience to be missed.

Perhaps we meet a hot babe and fall in love; how can you argue with that? Maybe falling in love leads to marriage. Maybe a marriage proposal leads to talk of kids and raising a family. This is, after all, a path laden with social overlay and compliance.

With marriage and a family come the responsibilities of a steady job and putting food on the table. Many of us take on jobs we don't like; jobs that don't challenge us; jobs we literally dislike. We do it because we're responsible and accountable. We do it because we've made choices and now we have to live with them.

Often, we forget about our physical health and allow ourselves to get out of shape. We forget about our mental health and give up the things that once stimulated us. Sometimes, we ignore our spirituality.

Suddenly, we're dealing with the dreams and aspirations of the young ones that we brought into this world and our focus changes. These things take work. They take energy. In one sense, we are building our legacies, or some semblance of our legacies. But in another sense, the legacy of the man who wanted to run for President or live in Paris for a year has been put on a back burner or, worse, has been purged from our list of important things altogether.

Who was that guy anyway? Can he be the same guy who comes home from a long day at the office, pours a drink for himself, and settles down in front of the television? This man is stuffing his pain deep down inside. Can he be the same guy who spends his weekends taking his kids to soccer games and, with any luck, gets in nine holes of golf?

———

The truth is that complacency is the enemy of every man (or woman) whose vision of self has been blurred by the dictates of everyday living.

———

I'm not trying to inflict a new way of thinking on anyone; if you've found a completely satisfying life, I

46

commend you. But if you've ever had even a momentary pause when you've thought, "Is this all there is?" then I think revisiting your "inner Aconcagua" is a worthwhile endeavor.

Suggesting that you, I, or anyone else should aspire to become a complete person is not an indictment against the person you are at the moment. Suggesting that you, I, or anyone else might want to push ourselves to greater heights in the workplace is not a reflection on where we are with our businesses right now. Suggesting that you, I, or anyone else can be a better friend, partner, or lover is not a condemnation of what we offer to our relationships today.

——

But to deny the itch to step further out onto the ledge of fulfillment, adventure, or uncertainty is not what any of us really want to do. And if we do, where does that leave us? Stuck. Complacent. Fearful.

——

There is not a man among us who doesn't have a powerful purpose to live up to. There is not a man among us who doesn't want to travel the unexplored roads of our imaginations. And more deeply, those parts of ourselves are lingering there, like a day slowly slipping into night. Many of us do not pay attention to that feeling of deep dissatisfaction as we go to sleep at night.

I say, "Be freaked out about the death of your dreams. Be freaked out about not exploring that part of yourself."

There is a gap that too many of us don't bridge, and that is the gap between doing what we see as responsible and accountable to others—like taking care of our families

47

and providing a certain lifestyle—and being integral and accountable to ourselves. But here is something I can guarantee you. The man who is willing to ask, "What do I really want out of life?" and the man who is prepared to go after what he really wants out of life will, in the end, be a better partner, a better father, and a better human being. Can you hear that?

The problem with complacency is this. Too often, something will show up in our world—an opportunity will present itself; maybe even the opportunity of a lifetime like the Aconcagua Project—and many of us don't know how to navigate it. We may even choose to ignore it as an opportunity.

———

These opportunities can and should be a wake-up call. These opportunities should be screaming in your ear: What is my primary directive?

———

That is exactly how Dennis Carruth, the oldest member of our team and a longtime real estate developer, saw the Aconcagua Project: he saw it as a wake-up call. He was facing the uncertainty of a real estate market that had clearly gone south. By his own admission, he was not really a real estate developer anymore, but rather an asset manager waiting for the market to turn around. He heard something inside that was saying, "I want more." Something new; something that would revive his passion, the way ski racing and fatherhood always had in the past. He saw Aconcagua as a quest with long-term ramifications beyond merely summiting a mountain; he saw it as a path to self-discovery.

In our discussions leading up to the project concerning whether he was ready to commit or not, I asked him bluntly, "What is going to be different in your life a year from now, if you don't do something different? " And Dennis got it.

What sense did it make to take time away from his business? Did it make sense to invest the money? What about the time involved in training his body for the climb? And for each question, the answer was always the same: he knew he wanted to create a powerful future for himself. The answer was always no, it does not make sense logically. But it made sense to his soul.

———

**The first step is to stop being so "reasonable" about your life. Stop being a victim to society's rules of mediocrity and complacency.
Quit adapting to the dictates of society and start using society for your benefit.**

———

What about fear?

I ask the question because fear is always a big part of stepping up to something new and different: seizing an opportunity above and beyond the ordinary; challenging the status quo that the world has created for us. The good news is that fear is not a bad thing at all. Fear is a sign that we're challenging our comfort zones, and challenging our comfort zones is essential if we want to grow and change in a positive way. The really good news is that once you can see fear as a positive thing, taking action is a natural by-product.

Hell, yes, there were fearful moments as the seven of us contemplated the time, money, and effort it would take to commit to the Aconcagua Project. Every one of us had to process what we were considering and who and what it would affect. I, myself, had to overcome any number of fears and obstacles in convincing myself to move forward with the project at the outset. Then I asked the question: What is the primary directive in my life?

My directive is learning and growing as a man. If I want to learn and grow, will this project assist me in doing that? I invite each of you, whether male or female, to ask the same question: What is my primary directive?

I also realized that the experience the project would ultimately create would inevitably be one of the greatest vehicles for learning that I might ever encounter, and not just for me, but for others as well. And any time we are learning, each of us has the potential—actually, even the responsibility—to share that learning.

That sharing is what I'd dedicated my life to as a leadership coach, a business consultant, and a man of spirit: to inspire people to recognize how they want to be in the world and what they want to do, and then how to take action to get there.

———

We all have the ability to influence others in the world: Every one of us can do so by being of service, creating change, and sharing the learning.

———

Those are not the words of complacency. Those are the words of action. Complacency, however, is easy.

Taking action with a focus on making positive changes in the world can be challenging.

_____

Trust me, there is great value in seminars and personal growth, but none of it means anything until there is some service-oriented action caused by the learning.

_____

This is not to criticize seminar work. I've conducted hundreds of seminars and participated in many others. They're good for sharing information and creating new frameworks for thought. But if a seminar doesn't lead to action in the real world, there is no value to it.

In a previous chapter, I shared how three members of our team—Troy, Jeff, and I—got lost coming down from the summit of James Peak in a whiteout.

When we were in the car going home that evening, Troy suddenly looked over at me and said, "I've decided I'm going to love people more."

That was amazing! I was moved to tears to hear such a proclamation coming from the mouth of this normally guarded engineer. I said, "What brought that out, buddy?"

"What happened up there on the mountain scared me," he replied. "I don't share how I feel about people. I never have. Well, I'm done with that. From now on, I'm going to open up more. I'm going to be open to sharing my feelings. And I'm going to feel more."

For Troy, the crisis situation on James Peak had been an epiphany: a moment of clarity. Those are the moments we treasure. And if we're not seeking them, then we have to stop and figure out why. What can we do to create moments of clarity and change, just as being lost at the top of a mountain did for Troy?

I, myself, came away from the experience on James Peak feeling just a little bit more alive. I woke up the next day feeling the lightness of the day. Even food tasted better. I was more eager to smile. I was more eager to embrace the day.

The obvious conclusion was to seek out experiences that reinforced those feelings. The experiences don't have to be precarious in nature, such as when a couple of poor decisions on James Peak put my safety at risk.

As I said in my book *Learning to Believe the Unbelievable*, you have to throw out your old script. That's one of my favorite and most valued tenets. Reasonable and comfortable are not the worst things in the world, unless it begins to cost us the experiences of the amazing and the joyful.

Okay, so what does it take to get there: to throw away your old story and begin to write some new pages for your life? The Greeks call it a "metanoia," or a positive psychological re-building, which surely includes growth and healing. Some of us call it an epiphany; something of such significance that you're jarred to think and act in new ways. Unless there is an epiphany or a metanoia, it is very difficult for transformation to occur. And the question that arises from that is this: what causes an epiphany? What causes a heart to open enough for someone to say, "I'm going to evolve."

I can tell you, from all I have seen and done, that there are two elements we should take note of.

For one thing, an epiphany or a "religious experience" cannot be planned. You can seek new levels of awareness and new experiences, but you can't plan that type of transformational metamorphosis. It is essentially unplanned.

Secondly, it cannot come from a place of comfort. You have to push yourself into areas of discomfort or into a willingness to feel "uncomfortable."

The unknown is an uncomfortable place. Shunning complacency can be uncomfortable. Admitting you're not the person you want to be can be uncomfortable. Risk is uncomfortable.

Let's look at the Aconcagua Project from that point of view.

There are dangers involved in taking on a mountain standing 22,843 feet above sea level, where 75 mph winds strafe the landscape, where zero degree temperatures are commonplace, where one wrong turn can send a man or woman plunging down a ravine, where altitude sickness, headaches, and lung ailments stop people in their tracks every day. A full seventy percent of the people who challenge the slopes of Aconcagua fail to make the summit.

Now it's safe to say that I didn't want anyone hurt or injured or, God forbid, killed during our climb.

But I knew, even before the project came together, that there was going to be suffering. And that came to fruition the very first Tuesday that we met up at Red Rocks Amphitheater for Eric Wiseman's first planned training session. We ran the stairs. We crab-walked the stairs. We did crunches on the stage and pull-ups on the crossbeams. We did intervals. We did burpees until we puked.

We hurt. We suffered. We probably asked ourselves why we were subjecting our bodies to this: sweat burning our eyes and heartbeats racing at 185 beats a minutes.

Leave it to me to ask the inevitable question. "What," I asked during one of many water breaks, "is the value in suffering?"

And leave it to Dennis, our elder statesman, to have an answer. "It's freeing," he said.

Some part of Dennis could really see that there was something freeing in pushing his limits. The physical exertion had a freeing effect on his psyche and his spirit. This was a remarkable discovery. This was the place of epiphany.

So despite the pain and suffering, we committed ourselves to returning twice a week for six months for the same regimen. Work, suffer, and push our limits. Get stronger. Become more and more aware.

5 THE POWER OF PHYSICALITY

Human beings aren't built to sit in front of computers. We're not designed physically to vegetate in front of a video game for hours on end or watch back-to-back movies on our flat-screen televisions. We aren't meant to earn our livings sitting in cubicles for eight-hour-stretches.

———

Human beings were designed and built to move.

———

Our lives up until the last century reflected this, for the most part. We spent our days farming or hunting. We spent our days cultivating our fields or tracking game. We were on our feet. We walked into town. We walked to the mailbox. We moved. Even when the Industrial Revolution began, most men worked in jobs that kept them on their feet; kept them in motion.

Physicality earned us the right to sit around the dinner table after a day spent on our feet, yes, but this physicality also helped keep our minds clear and our focus concentrated. Movement helped keep us young, even when our diets were not optimum. The more physicality one has in his or her life, the more clarity there is around mental, emotional, and spiritual needs.

Our world changed when technology hit in a big way. You could probably take this back as far as the introduction of the automobile, but let's stay more current. Technology, even though most of us see it as valuable and accommodating, has nonetheless fermented a more sedentary society. The more sedentary your life in the workplace is, the more apt you are to spend your leisure time sitting as well. It's even believed that the current epidemic of sleep disorders can be attributed to the fact that too many of us, me included, spend too much time in a chair. Not surprisingly, our diet suffers. Our lives can become numb.

_____

Physicality is one of the prime tools we have at our disposal. Tying a physical commitment to a larger goal opens the door to a world of possibility.

_____

When the Aconcagua team came together, we understood from the outset that our training would be extensive. We knew that we would be pushing ourselves to be in the best shape of our lives. We knew it would take a regular training regimen as a team, clawing our way up the stairs at Red Rocks, scaling 14,000 foot peaks in some extreme conditions, changing our diets where necessary, and getting up at the crack of dawn to get in individual roadwork or treadmill time.

However, I also made it clear at the outset that part of our commitment to the project would include regular forays into areas such as leadership, service, change, mentoring, teaching, and listening. We would talk about some seemingly untouchable topics such as "what it means to be a man" in an era when more and more men are being accused of getting soft, acquiescing when they should be giving their own needs more attention, and seeking approval from all the wrong sources.

What was it that we wanted? We dubbed this goal the search for our "inner Aconcagua," the symbol of our search for something deeper; something more relevant, revelatory, and fulfilling beyond where we were when the process began in June.

Our goal was a metanoia that would truly signal transformation in both our personal and professional lives.

The thing to remember is this. The more fit you are, the stronger you feel mentally. And the better your conditioning, the more plugged in you are emotionally, and the more comfortable you are exploring your spirituality. Just as important is the fact that your view of what you can do in the world changes. Your view of what you can do in the world expands. You feel more powerful and loving. Suddenly, there are fewer limits. Suddenly, you no longer find yourself making excuses.

This is one key to self-leadership. The types of physical and mental exercises that we're discussing, and the forays into the growth of our spiritual and emotional realms, have to be done "mindfully." Not haphazardly or blindly, but with vigilance and attentiveness. The man who is mindful of his actions is far more likely to experience the change of heart that we've been talking about. For our Aconcagua team, that meant seeking the "virtual" summit above and beyond the 22,834-foot summit of the actual mountain.

Confidence is one more extraordinarily important by-product of being physically fit. For men in particular, the extrapolation of being in shape and growing confident in our personal and professional lives is unmistakable.

Now this is not to say that it is impossible for a person to achieve a high level of mental and spiritual awareness without first taking steps to become physically fit. There are plenty of stories of monks or ascetics who spend their lives in a monastery or cave and find illumination. And, of course, there are many happy and contented people who have never taken more than a short walk. Both the monk and the inactive man or woman can and often do live their lives with integrity and honor. No one would question that. And from my experience, men and women who get involved in life and choose to serve and contribute tend to be very happy and fulfilled human beings.

The Aconcagua Project had service and contribution, as well as energy and drive, as its foundation, so a commitment to the physical was essential. And in addition to that, I wanted each member of our team to see himself as a man with the capacity to lead and influence, to teach and mentor, to inspire and motivate.

———

In the past, these were the people we referred to as "gurus." But the day of the guru is over. In my view, we all have the capacity to teach

through how we live our lives.

─────

If you and I are waiting for someone in some high and mighty place to save the day in a world with enormous problems and a society with questionable values, then we are in big trouble. It's not going to happen.

The President of our country, whether you approve or disapprove of his politics, cannot save our economy or educate our kids; he cannot create a moral base from which we should all live or convince us that we live on a planet worth loving.

While there are religious leaders and philosophers who may very well offer inspiration and even some degree of enlightenment, they cannot change the values of six and a half billion people.

While there are business leaders many of us admire, who may have broad-based influence, they cannot single-handedly conquer poverty or bring about an end to unemployment.

─────

The only people who can "save the day" or truly inspire change are you and me as individuals.

─────

We do this with the actions we take day to day, the people we reach out to, and the decisions we consciously make. We do this by finding where our integrity lives and then being vigilant about it.

We all have to create some type of movement, big or small, that has as its end game a world that is a better place to live in than it is today. Mine is a grassroots approach toward collaborative leadership that begins with each of us getting our own lives straightened out first and foremost: being responsible to our families, being responsible to the workplace, being responsible to our communities, being self-referential.

It's simple: if you take care of yourself first, you can then offer a hand in taking care of the world. This is the philosophy at the heart of the Aconcagua Project. Begin with self—find out what you want to be and what you're willing to do to get there—and then the reaching out that you do to the world will have real substance.

Today's leaders, in particular on the political side of things, have not done this. Many are, at best, what I call "wobbly." They don't really know themselves. As sad and disappointing as it is, solving the problems of the day and focusing on the issues of our nation are not at the top of their priority list. Satisfying their fundraisers is. Keeping the guy on the other side of the aisle down is. Winning re-election is. Suddenly they find themselves living outside of their integrity, maybe because they never identified where their integrity lived in the first place.

What is integrity? In part, it means being true to your word no matter what the cost is.

If I promise myself that I will get up at six o'clock in the morning and walk around my neighborhood for twenty minutes, and that's what I do, then I'm living in my integrity. Take that example and expand upon it a hundred-fold. Then imagine the power and velocity in your life once you have fortified your integrity. Doing what we say we will do impacts everything in our lives. It's really that simple. It's not about breaking a promise to someone else; integrity comes from within, and you know when you've left that place. You will know it. You can hide from it, but you will still be aware of it.

I know this. If I make a promise to myself everyday to take some sort of action or live up to some level of behavior, and I follow through with those promises, I will find myself behaving differently in the world. Those promises that we make to ourselves are the building blocks of the epiphany we've been talking about. Those are the makings of a life of leadership.

Let's say a client comes to see me and says, "My goal is to start an import company and earn $500,000 a year." This client also tells me that her current income is $100,000 a year. While making that quantum leap from $100,000 to $500,000 seems aggressive, it is also doable. It hinges on one thing: my client keeping her word to herself without exception.

I might say to her at the end of our first session, "Okay, go home and write a blog about the five most important steps a person has to take before importing textiles from India. Send it to me tomorrow. And don't promise me you'll do it. Promise yourself."

This may seem like a simple thing to do. But it's not the simplicity. It's the act. It's saying you're going to do something and following through. All success is based upon that: keeping promises to yourself.

There are two clear-cut paths; two very identifiable constructs. You either believe in yourself, or you don't believe in yourself. Again, it sounds so simple, doesn't it? If the client in this example is just saying she wants to earn a half-million dollars a year, but doesn't truly believe it, it will never happen.

On the other side of the coin is a person with such velocity and power in her own word and in her own integrity that her belief is inherent. The promise of that one blog leads to a second promise, a second step, a second action item; a thousand kept promises down the road and she is seeing her goal of a $500,000 yearly income and a thriving business as a reality. These things are not mysterious; we just make them a mystery.

———

**When you believe in yourself, you find a way.
All things come to pass
for the man or woman who believes.**

———

The members of the Aconcagua team made this promise to one another. As part of our training, we would commit to climbing a series of 14,000-foot peaks in Colorado's incomparable Rocky Mountains over a five-month period.

We took on the first of these on August 5ᵗ after two months of group and individual training. Our goal was a trio of peaks just northwest of the town of Alma, Colorado: Mounts Democrat, Lincoln, and Bross.

Eric, our high altitude trainer, chose these three peaks because they were considered a fairly easy one-day climb, given the fact that we were all showing signs of getting in shape. These Peaks are located in the north-westernmost corner of Pike National Forest, as beautiful a place as you can find and only a ninety-minute drive from Denver.

We were only a team of six at this point, since Vince had yet to join us. Troy, Eric, Greg, and I traveled west from Denver, while Jeff and Dennis made the trek from their respective abodes in Glenwood Springs and Aspen.

The road out of Alma traveled past the remnants of silver mining operations long since depleted, and we rendezvoused a mile from Kite Lake at the crossroads of an old, deserted mining road. We set out just after eight o'clock in the morning.. We skirted Kite Lake and used an old road that gradually rose to a well-defined trail at the foot of our grand and stately trio.

We carried backpacks, but they were nothing compared to the loads we would hoist up the slopes of Aconcagua. Still, a 14,000 peak is still a worthy trek—ask any Coloradoan who has ever tackled one—and soon enough we were well above tree line and staring at the saddle between Mounts Democrat and Lincoln.

Not long thereafter, we crested Democrat's summit, a full 14,148 feet above sea level, and found ourselves with a view of staggering dimensions. We could see as far as the tailings pond for the Climax Mine near the top of Fremont Pass in one direction and all the way to Pike's Peak in the other.

We didn't tarry long, however, and dropped down to the saddle between Democrat and Cameron—a loss of about 750 vertical feet—and took a short break to hydrate and nourish.

For me, this climb represented a unique opportunity to observe the team dynamics in a less controlled environment than our normal training sessions. These were guys used to taking charge in the workplace, and yet here it was about working together, enjoying the camaraderie, and getting to know each other in an unfamiliar setting.

We pressed on. The climb to the top of Mount Cameron followed a thousand-foot-long ridge. There was less loose rock here than we had encountered on Democrat, but the wind was far chiller. Near the summit, the trail crossed to the northwest side of the ridge, increasing our exposure to the elements, but the footing was good and there was really no danger of slipping off the side of the mountain.

We were now at an elevation of 14,239 feet with a view that made me appreciate how extraordinarily blessed we were to be living with the Rockies in our backyards. I was with five men who felt very much the same, and I could see the effect on their faces and hear it in their laughter.

But the wind, always a factor at altitude, got our feet moving, and we headed northeast for a half mile toward the summit of Mount Lincoln, a mere forty-seven feet higher than Cameron! We forged a quasi-false summit, scrambled through a mini rock field, and had the summit all to ourselves. We ate and drank again and gave thanks for our good fortune.

With the threat of weather heading our way from across the divide, we traversed an old mining road across the north side of Mount Bross and forged a half-dozen switchbacks to the fortress-like summit and a vista of astounding proportions. "It's like standing on top of the world," someone said, and I had to wonder what it would be like staring out at the world from Aconcagua's 22,834-foot summit; a good 7,000 feet higher. There was also a tendril of anxiety I couldn't deny.

6 MAN IN RELATIONSHIP WITH WOMEN

The real beauty of men and women is the polarity that exists between them. This polarity is defined by the wonderful differences between male and female: physically, yes, but also our mental, emotional, and spiritual differences. Our definitions of success and failure can't possibly be the same, but both genders can benefit from the others' perspective.

Unfortunately, it is this wonderful polarity that has taken a beating lately. It doesn't benefit society to try and fit both genders into the same mold; it does benefit society if we respect our differences and treasure our uniqueness.

What can we as men and women do about these differences?

The polarity between men and women is as much energetic as it is reflective of our sexual organs. The energetic and physical make-up of a man is to give while a woman receives. Men tend to thrive in challenge and women respond to a feeling of security. Men that are ungrounded and uncertain do not provide the experience of security in their relationships with women. Then women in their quest to become secure can become man-like and

65

men can soften in this juxtaposed polarity. It leaves men and women confused, and, seemingly, the polarity is neutralized. Then there is no romance or respect for one another. The easier things are, the softer we get. The softer we get, the more comfortable we feel. Unfortunately, growth and change do not hinge upon comfort: in fact, just the opposite. Growth and change come center stage the more we are challenged and the more discomfort we feel. As men and women, we are inspired when we grow.

———

**And here is the thing we so often miss:
if we aren't growing, we are not happy.**

———

Men and women are built differently and, too often, we are trying to be the same. Stagnation and the status quo are killers. They kill our drive at work. They make it harder for us to see that hardship is just a stepping-stone toward success. And they kill the energy that every relationship we develop needs in order to stay healthy, whether it's at work, at home, or in the community.

If we're not growing, we're not fulfilled.

Here's a great example. Look at those men or women who have won the lottery. Then look at the statistics which reveal the strain and the unhappiness that often haunts these people, and ask, for what reason? There was no challenge. Some part of these people seems to sabotage what we all imagine would be a walk down easy street. But there's that word again. Easy. Easy isn't the answer. The harder the challenge is, the more satisfying the result and the more defining the transformation.

Every time the Aconcagua team takes to the steps of Red Rocks Amphitheater, climbing stairs until our muscles burn, there is a sense of real accomplishment. And we know when we hit the arduous slopes of the great mountain itself; we'll very likely be the strongest climbers out there.

So if you are a man reading this book, and you have been avoiding challenge, consider the power and possibility that lies in creating a project that forces you into your leadership again.

How many people work all their lives toward a retirement with no substance? "I want to retire so I can go fishing every day." "I can't wait to retire so we can travel at our leisure." We all know people like this, and rarely does it lead to happiness.

Entitlement has the same affect, whether we're talking about people who spent their entire lives milking a welfare system that rewards their idleness, or people who think their station in life somehow accords them respect they haven't earned.

———

When you're not offering anything to the world, it's hard to be happy. It's as simple as that. Or maybe it's as complicated as that.

———

Men need to be challenged. We need to challenge ourselves. We need to reestablish the wonderful polarity between men and women, not try to dissolve it the way certain misguided movements suggest we should.

So how do we do that? How do we find our Aconcagua? How do we find that challenge that pushes us to a place where we get up in the morning excited to face the day and feeling just a little uncomfortable because we're facing something new and different? We've all heard the famous Joseph Campbell line: Follow your bliss. Okay, great. But what the hell does that mean?

In my experience, we freeze-frame a single word from the previous paragraph: *excited*.

What excites you? What gets your juices flowing just by thinking about it and maybe even gets the butterflies dancing in your stomach?

It could be anything. It could be scuba diving or fly-fishing. It could be quitting your job and plunging into a new business. It could be breaking free of a worn-out relationship or doing something to re-create a worn-out relationship?

We all have something that moves us; that excites us, which lives at the edge of our conscious minds urging us to jump. But too few of us do anything about it. We like easy. We like feeling safe. Why do we like that? The reasons are many: because it takes effort, because we're afraid, or because we're comfortable.

I love talking to people about making their lives better. I enjoy talking to people about the evolution of their lives, their businesses, and their perspectives. That's my business. I walked away from banking eighteen years ago and dedicated myself to the creation of leaders. I determined that I could do that by coaching people to find

68

the thing that inspires them. That is what gets me juiced up.

Beyond this work, I've discovered a love of the outdoors: hiking, climbing, and skiing. One of my first Aconcagua moments was an extraordinary trip to Chile with my brother Douglas, leading a group of hardy souls on a ten-day, white-water rafting adventure down the Rio Futa river. I expected the same life-changing experience when we had tackled Aconcagua.

———

**Maybe learning new things excites you
as much as it does me.
If so, how do we facilitate this?**

———

Reading books works, but maybe taking a class at the local community college is a better way to make you feel that sense of enthusiasm that we discussed earlier. Exploring the Internet is easy and fun, but maybe planning a research trip in your area of interest—the rise and fall of the financial markets, for instance—would be the thing that puts the "challenge" back in your life and stretches your boundaries. That's what growth is.

How does this serve the polarity we're discussing? If you look at our very simple examples, it's a pretty safe bet that the class at the community college will begin filling your personal well with new information and new insight. Try sharing this "newness" with your significant other, and watch the results. Let's say your research trip takes you to New York City to observe the Stock Exchange in action. How can you not come home from an experience like that as a different person? There is a very good chance that your significant other will find this different person even more attractive than the person who left.

That's the gift of exploring the new and different. Exploration adds to our experience, which fuels our perspective. Our individual perspectives add dynamics to our relationships and make the polarity between the sexes even healthier.

It's not attractive to be stuck in the mud. And it's not attractive when the polarity between you and the woman in your life narrows.

———

You don't need to be a wealthy person by society's standards. Growth is wealth. Learning is wealth. And sharing that with other people is the surest of all signs of wealth: wealth of spirit, wealth of purpose, and wealth of commitment.

———

One of the biggest and most important facets of any man's life is who we choose as our partners. Why can some guys meet a girl at eighteen, date for a period of time, marry, and stay married for fifty years? And why do some guys, at thirty, meet and marry someone who they divorce three years later?

The question in either case is how well we know ourselves as men and as people. I confess that I didn't know myself at all when I married for the first time, even though that didn't become really obvious to me until much later.

Indeed, the road we each travel is uniquely our own. No two men (or women) navigate the same path. However, asking that one simple question is powerful beyond words.

How well do I know myself?

If a man doesn't really know himself, how can he choose a partner that fulfills not only the physical dynamics of the relationship, but also the mental, emotional, and spiritual dynamics? He can't. And since so many men among us are in that boat—women too, to be honest—perhaps that leads to the unfortunate demise of so many relationships. And the fact is that many of us, including yours truly, have quit relationships when they became hard. If you don't know yourself, it's hard to respect yourself. And if you don't respect yourself, it's going to be very hard to respect and love someone else.

If I were able to turn back the clock, would I choose not to have married when and whom I did? The answer is an emphatic no. What I learned about myself and other people during the course of my marriage, and every day since we called it quits, has given extraordinary substance to my life and made me better prepared for subsequent relationships. It was all part of getting to know myself.

There is a problem. Most men cannot really see our own "stuff," our own hang-ups, or our bad habits. We're blind to them.

Maybe that's why men's groups are so effective and why too few men belong to them. Who wants to have their hang-ups and bad habits pointed out to them? Well, only those of us who want to get to know ourselves better.

71

I have someone in my life that helps me to see myself more clearly.

I have a coach that I see twice each month in Phoenix, Arizona named Steve Hardison. He is an amazing man. His website is www.TheUltimateCoach.net. Steve was kind enough one day to point out to me that in all relationships there is chemistry and there is workability. In my past, I have had relationships that were all chemistry and little workability and vice versa. I may have loved the person I was in a relationship with in each of those cases, but that didn't mean that we could create a life together.

I have since learned that when you find a reasonable balance of chemistry and workability with the woman in your life —and it's never a perfect balance—then you have a relationship with a future. I have also learned that who I am being as a man will determine the success or failure of any relationship I have. It begins with a deep-seated commitment to myself and with a powerful projection of that commitment into the relationship.

If I cannot commit to my own life, then how the hell can I powerfully commit to a marriage? Once again, this is about knowing yourself. How do you define workability? What are the things in a relationship that are important to you? You will not know those things until you really know yourself. How do you get to know yourself? By applying the concepts that I have been talking about in this book and that were manifested in the Aconcagua Man Project.

And then there is chemistry, sexual attraction, and romance. If I am not living my life wide fucking open, how will I possibly attract a woman that is equally alive and vital? I won't.

Remember this also. It can't be all about physical attraction and sex, though these are major factors. What about humor? What about intellectual stimulus? What about mutual interests? These cannot be faked, and they cannot be denied.

––––––

The better you and I know ourselves, the easier it is to serve the world around us. And the more we serve the world around us, the more likely we are to do work that we love.

––––––

When that happens, we're not asking anyone's approval. We are moving forward with an eye on something important; something that moves us. And when we're moved by something, everything around us is positively influenced, including our relationships with the women in our lives.

Too many men think that loving is weak and that showing love is a sign of weakness. In fact, the truth is much more profound.

––––––

Love is most powerful source of energy that we have. Nothing else even comes close.

––––––

Too many men don't have a clear idea of what love is.

Love is acceptance. Love is owning self. It's not about apologizing or accepting less than you expect. Love is about respect; love is about showing respect, and it is also about being respectful. Love is about being accountable. Love is about holding others accountable.

Love is about allowing others to be themselves; your significant other most importantly. Love is also about finding situations where being yourself is the ultimate gift.

Perhaps most importantly, love is a behavior. I do not always need to feel like loving someone as much as I need to demonstrate love.

7 INNER ALIGNMENT

Many people will look at the Aconcagua Man Project as merely an attempt to summit a mountain. Of course, it's more than that, as we have been saying throughout these pages. Climbing the mountain is our "outer" journey. But there is an even more important "inner" journey that makes this more visible outer journey possible.

As esoteric as this might sound to the ears of a lot of men, it just happens to be true.

In all cases, in the pursuit of whatever your Aconcagua might be, it is always the "inner" journey driving the "outer" journey.

———

More clarity at the "self" level translates naturally into more clarity at the "service" level.

———

Men thrive on service.

For example, a man creates a non-profit organization, and he takes pleasure in having done something powerful for the world. A man helps a neighbor plant a tree in his backyard, and he feels a real sense of himself. He doesn't do these things for money, position, or power; he does them because serving others brings us, as men, more alive.

Take the Aconcagua project. The very decision to commit to the project, the preparation, the climb, and the integration of everything we experienced began as an inner decision.

In the world of effective leadership, the pursuit of an outer goal without inner alignment doesn't work. It just doesn't. The most salient example is the one we hear most often quoted. If your overriding goal in starting a new business is to become fabulously wealthy—and I'm not saying there's anything wrong with being wealthy—then your odds of failure are the kind of odds that get the people in Las Vegas salivating. You might as well hang out a sign that says: No chance. My motivation is all out of whack.

Here's a straightforward statement: I have a goal. I want to build a skyscraper on Manhattan Island and blow the roof off the real estate market. Why? What is driving this goal? What is going on inside me that makes me want to undertake this endeavor? What is my primary directive?

If, at the end of the day, I find myself staring up at my creation feeling as empty inside as the building is even before my tenants begin to move in, then what?

———

The truth is men can be very stupid. We often want what we've been told we should want. We've been told what we should want by society, by our teachers, by our parents, or by whomever. The trick to living a meaningful life is to ask the question: What is my Aconcagua?

———

All of these well-meaning sources have an image of what a man is supposed to be and what a man should want. And you and I, too often, buy in to it. We're products of long-standing perceptions that everyone expects us to adopt and even embrace. Get a job—even if it's one you hate—support your family, find an easy chair that fits you, and retire as early as possible.

Very seldom does someone say, "Look inside. Find out what you want. Embrace being an individual. Trust yourself." Not many people ever say, "Make sure you take some big risks in your life, because living on your edge will reap rewards on the inner and outer levels of life." Probably, no one has ever said, "Your legacy lives on without you, so make sure it's the legacy you want."

So the question becomes: how do I live on the edge? Clearly, it's not by listening to the chatter of society.

The answer is, you explore. You make yourself feel uncomfortable by stepping into uncharted territory. You allow yourself to rise up or fall.

Here is one of the few guarantees I can make. If you get up and do something that makes you uncomfortable, uncertain, or anxious, you'll inevitably come away from the event a slightly different man. And you should do this not just once, but on a regular basis. You make the commitment, and then you follow through, because you said you would. You live up to your word, without fail. And if you do fail—which we all do sometimes—you clean up your mess and move on to the next risky endeavor.

77

―――

**Access to evolution as a man comes through
pushing for consistent "discomfort"
and learning to love it.**

―――

Yes, "evolution" is a new word here and so fitting. Evolution is what the Aconcagua team signed up for, and not just for one training exercise or one coaching session. And not just for one hike or one leadership roundtable. Instead, it was for nine months' worth of training and coaching, and dozens of hikes and continuous conversations about leadership.

Society wants you to believe that you can have that new, totally fit body in just ten minutes a day: just turn on the television and a dozen infomercials will show you how. Society wants you to believe that you can achieve monumental wealth by attending a seminar on options trading; just turn on the television, and you'll find any number of financial gurus dying to tell you how. We all know that it doesn't happen that way. We all know that it's an illusion. But do we know why it's an illusion? It's because there is no evolution involved: no wisdom, no sacrifice, and therefore, no growth. Growth equates to evolution. Being evolved as a man can determine the true fulfillment of your life.

Let me give you a physical example of a commitment to evolve. Part of my workout routine in preparation for the climb up Aconcagua was something called the Spartan 300.

You may have heard of it. If not, the routine goes like this:

- ≅ Pull-ups - 25 reps
- ≅ Deadlifts with 135 lbs. - 50 reps
- ≅ Pushups - 50 reps
- ≅ 24-inch box jumps - 50 reps
- ≅ Abdominal floor wipers while benching 135 pounds - 50 reps
- ≅ Single-arm clean-and-press with 36 lbs. kettlebell - 50 reps
- ≅ Pull-ups - 25 reps.

You have to do it all in twenty minutes. It's brutal. And some part of me loves it. I come away from that workout ready to take on the world, ready to serve, ready to make a difference. Here's the thing. We all know that it's easier to vegetate in front of the television than it is to drive down to the community center and try to make a difference in some kid's life. But what's the downside? The downside is that there is no payoff. There never is when we take the easy way out.

The payoff comes from the other side, the side we're calling evolution.

On the other side of " uncomfortability" is tremendous evolution for any man or woman, and that is the upside.

And what is joy but an integral part of happiness? We're all seeking happiness.

79

Here was the Aconcagua team carrying full packs up the slopes of Grizzly Peak, snow drifts pushing against us every step of the way, and pitching our tents on the summit under a sky so clear and so piercingly beautiful that words couldn't possibly describe it. The moon was a huge disk hovering above us and illuminating the snow like fields of diamonds. It was a moment of sheer joy; I could feel it deep in my soul. And while I might have had a taste of that feeling by standing on my back porch looking at the same moon, the struggle that it took to reach the top of that peak turned it into an unforgettable event.

Inner alignment, the concept we began this chapter with, is a by-product of that sort of feeling. And the more life-altering moments that we create, the sounder that inner alignment becomes. It's not one-stop shopping. It's a course of action, a way of life, and a willingness to embrace how we evolve as human beings.

———

Deep down inside, we know that we grow by living on the edge.

———

Men want to be tempered. They want to be courageous.

Deep down, men know that vitality, achievement, and that sense of joy that we just mentioned are products of effort, hard work, and resolve. We know that inner alignment is the thing that drives the outer journey that we all are so eager to embark upon.

Picture a man who has a boss that he loathes: a boss that he can't bring himself to approach, a boss who wants nothing more than to keep him small and quiet. Maybe

80

he's having trouble paying his mortgage, has kids in school, and has a wife with a part-time job that isn't bringing in much money.

He has ideas he feels are viable, but he's afraid to voice them. He wants to take initiative, but he feels invisible. This is his Aconcagua; the mountain he has to climb. Does he risk his job by knocking on his boss's door and saying, "I have some ideas I want to share at our next managers' meeting. I think you'll like them. And I think they'll serve the company well."

Why wouldn't he share with his boss in this way? Maybe it's because he's a prisoner of fear, or because he's lost sight of his own integrity. There are lots of reasons, and we're all susceptible to them.

One of the hardest, most rewarding decisions that I ever had to make was to leave corporate America, to say, "I don't enjoy being a banker. I want something more." To take that leap of faith and believe there was something better on the other side. Talk about being a prisoner of fear. It took me two years, from the time I knew it was over, to actually take the leap.

I had a boss with a drinking problem. He was also a man with an inferiority complex, which, not surprisingly, led to a misuse, if not downright abuse, of power. He'd drag the gang out for a drink at the local pub at three o'clock in the afternoon, and the party would often still be going on at nine o'clock that night.. He'd order round after round on the company credit card and expect us to keep up.

One night, I was halfway through my first beer and staring at three more waiting in front of me. My best friend Todd and I had plans for dinner that night, and he showed up right about then. I was putting on my jacket when my boss looked at me and said, "If you don't finish those fucking beers, you won't have a job come morning."

I actually chugged one of the beers before Todd intervened and said, "Stephen, you don't need to do this."

He was right. I didn't need to do that. That wasn't me. So I left the beers sitting on the table and walked out. The next day my boss insisted that he had just been kidding. He hadn't. But it didn't matter. I had finally seen the light and conquered the fear. Every man or woman reading this has reached a time in life when we made the choice to speak our truth. We are only hostages to situations if we let that happen in our own minds, and finding our own Aconcagua will also assist in finding our own voice.

For me, at that moment, I was bound and determined to find work I loved.

Rest assured that there are a lot of men (and women) in America leading lives of quiet desperation. Yes, this is the same phrase made famous by Henry David Thoreau when he said, "Most men lead lives of quiet desperation and go to the grave with the song still in them."

Those are some of the most powerful words ever said, and they speak directly to our discussion about knowing yourself and being willing to step away from what everyone else thinks you should be.

———

Quiet desperation is no way to lead your life.

———

No one, man or woman, wants to go to the grave with the song still in them. We were born to discover our voice and to sing our song at the top of our lungs.

82

Thoreau also said this, "Go confidently in the direction of your dreams. Live the life you have imagined."

I couldn't agree more. But remember this: dreams require action. You can't just imagine, and you can't just hope. Hope is like trying to hold water in the palm of your hand. You have to pursue your talents. You have to do the work.

Climbing a mountain like Aconcagua requires many things. A love of blue skies and snowy venues surely doesn't hurt. Neither does a passion to feel the blood pumping through your veins. You may not be able to generate a love of nature, but you can become fit. And the fitter you are, the more willing you are to walk, run, and hike. Maybe the love of nature is just waiting to be discovered.

But climbing Aconcagua is not a technical feat; you don't have to be a skilled mountaineer like our teammate Vince, a high-level ski racer like Dennis, or a highly competitive athlete like Greg Aden. Commitment, determination, and persistence are the most essential skills, but then commitment, determination, and persistence are essential skills in nearly every endeavor that we undertake.

———

Slow down. Listen.
What do you hear?
What is your song?
What is your Aconcagua?
What is that thing that leaves
you inspired to live fully?

———

When you step out on that ledge of "evolution," you're suddenly learning things about yourself that go hand in hand with your inner alignment. And that's where the journey begins. That's when you get up off the couch and call your college buddy to start that new software company in your garage.

But don't get up off the couch and call your buddy because you think you should or because society says to. Do it because it will add value to your life and possibly to millions of others as well. Do it because it excites you, because you've discovered, or rediscovered, a sense of enthusiasm for your own evolution.

When I got the Aconcagua team rolling in June, one of the first things we talked about was creating something bigger than just an expedition to Argentina. We talked about putting something in motion that went beyond our training and preparation: something that could have an impact on others.

In the beginning, I didn't see it happening. The climb itself was a lot to put on anyone's plate. Then to add on to that endeavor a project that could positively impact others was asking a lot. But that wasn't an excuse I was willing to accept. Leadership, when all is said and done, is about results. It's also true that an effective leader has a vision, creates milestones for that vision, and inspires the overall purpose of any project or movement.

**That's all very lofty-sounding rhetoric,
but we all know that it doesn't mean a damn thing
if there aren't results at the end of the road.**

At times in my life, I have really pissed people off as a means of getting them off their rear ends, and I confess that I'm willing to do that if it serves a person who is trying to make some progress on his or her own objectives in life. I did that one Tuesday night during one of our team meetings. We were all gathered at my office, and Jeff Patterson was on the phone from his home in Glenwood Springs. I wasn't particularly pleased with the direction of our conversation. Here we were ignoring the inner alignment that was the entire point of this chapter.

What was the Aconcagua Man Project committed to? What was our purpose? Was it just about climbing a mountain?

Here was an appropriate time for me to remember that leadership was not always a matter of patting someone on the back. So, in essence, I said, "Are we going to be satisfied with just climbing a mountain, or are we going to try and do something going forward as a team in service of the world?"

I was, of course, talking about an endeavor that would open up the Aconcagua Man Project to a larger audience and produce a tangible agenda of service far beyond our actual climb. That's what the project was intended to do. This wasn't a surprise to anyone.

In other words, let's man up. Don't just say it, but act upon it.

In response to this "stirring of the pot," team member Greg Aden produced a blog on our web site www.TheAconcaguaProject.com that spelled it out for all of us. He called it: *The Purpose, My Purpose, Our Purpose.*

It read as follows:

As I really look into what the Aconcagua Man Project is all about and why I personally joined it, the following questions jump out. Where are my limits? What can I achieve personally, physically, spiritually, and emotionally if I truly apply all my learning AND train myself to listen to a higher calling? What/where is my true potential relative to service and inspiration to others?

Since this project started, I have experienced several positive changes, and I am recognizing that yes, I am becoming a better man. What this means in the long run and how it will impact those around me is still to be seen. For now, being true to myself and clear about what I want to create in life is my primary focus.

By combining the team element of the project and the power we all bring together as men makes the possibilities of helping others endless. Our mission is to serve other men: by reminding them to be real men; by inspiring them through sharing our story.

It is the intention of our team to do three things that will help the world.

1. *To inspire others by transparently sharing our journey.*
2. *To ask others to share their personal Aconcaguas.*
3. *To carry those stories to the top of Aconcagua, symbolically finishing the journey in their lives. Our goal is to carry 22,834 stories to the summit of Aconcagua. Why 22,834 sharings? Because Mount Aconcagua is 22,834 feet tall.*

Greg went further that same day. He dedicated himself to providing financial support through his own company to a number of charities, based upon our team hitting certain milestones throughout the climb. He also found several corporate and professional partners to match his donations and to raise awareness about the great work these charities were doing.

We said it earlier, but it's worth repeating. It is always the "inner" journey that ultimately drives the "outer" journey.

Today, I challenge you to gain clarity about what moves you and then explore it. If you are concerned about what others might think, you may never take action on your clarity. Forget what society thinks. Put a name to your own "Aconcagua" and take the first few steps toward the summit of your own success.

8 THE EVOLUTION OF THE TEAM

To be honest, I don't care a whole lot for the word "transformation."

It's a popular word these days, but it is one that is essentially misunderstood or misrepresented by people selling what I call "spiritual bypasses." I personally went through a real "woo-woo" phase in my life. I learned that saying something is not the same as doing it and that the words of leadership don't create anything. The sole determinant to performance is action.

What I am interested in—and what I would like you to consider—is the changing trajectory of a man or woman's life such that he or she can make a real difference in the world and come away with the ability to love his or her life in a truly electric way.

———

**A transformation is a slight alteration
in your view of the world.
Transformation is a moment in time.**

———

A man has to create those moments in time for himself. You have to be willing to put yourself on the line. But even more so, you have to be willing to step over the line into areas of life that are unfamiliar to you, into areas of interest that may scare you just a little, because you're not sure how effective you'll be or how successful. We called it "evolution" earlier. These are the moments in time that have to be compounded over and over again to create evolution of spirit, mind, and body. This is an evolution of consciousness that has you taking actions that in your past would not have been possible. What does this mean on a practical level?

From a physical perspective, you can go to the gym one time and find something transformational in lifting weights. You may say, "I've found something here that really makes me feel great. It does it for me." Excellent. But going once doesn't mean much a week down the road. If you're going to evolve physically, you have to make going to the gym a lifestyle. Then you're on the verge of evolution, and that's where your energy has to lie.

――――

**Evolution isn't easy. It takes dedication and a
commitment to doing
what you say you will do.**

――――

The Aconcagua team came off a brutally cold climb to the summit of James Peak in the Colorado Rockies, averted a potential disaster when Troy, Jeff, and I took a wrong turn off the mountain, and came away from the day with a new perspective. It was inevitable. That night, Troy shared a piece of what it was for him when he said, "I've

90

decided I'm going to love people more. I haven't been good about that up to now, and I'm going to allow myself to go there as often as possible."

That insight and commitment is nothing short of transformational. Yet, it is the task of following up on such a vibrant moment by discovering ways to live that statement every day that will propel Troy's growth, going forward.

We all face the same task in our development. If you think you can sit back and wait for these moments to drop from the heavens, then you're missing the message. You must act now because the planet needs you now.

The essence of great leadership is not the bundle of tools that creates far-reaching strategy. It's not the vision that you paint. It's not the ability to motivate people to buy into a project. It's not the direction that you give on a tactical level. Yes, those are essential elements, but the essence of successful leadership is, when all is said and done, results.

———

A lot of men in today's world are confused about what it really means to be a man; they're not clear exactly what the results are supposed to look like.

———

How can we be sensitive, but also strong? How can we be vulnerable, but also courageous? How can we act with purpose, but also leave room for flexibility?

When I was first "constructing" the Aconcagua team, I wanted men who were open to this exploration about what it really means to be a man. This was not, however,

91

solely about what they could extract from the process, but also included the value they could give to the process.

I wanted men who were amazing in their own way and generous in spirit, but who were also willing to explore the trajectory of their lives. Where were they going as men and people? How could they learn to love their lives? How could they be of more service? These were some of the many questions that we discussed during our initial team gathering.

I came right out with it. "Everyone in this room is amazing, or you wouldn't be here. Everyone in this room is generous, or you wouldn't be here either."

In the realm of effective leadership, this is called creating "a listening" for the group. You plant a seed of truth: not a seed of half-truths or wishful thinking. When people hear a proclamation deeming them "generous," they understand at some level that they have to be generous. When they've been declared "amazing," they feel they have to live up to that. It's a wonderful way of bringing out the best in people, because now they are hearing things about themselves that they may never have considered. That's uplifting.

Consider the antithesis of this. "You suck. Now prove me wrong." Not quite as effective, is it?

———

When a man or woman sees what he or she has to offer, that person will go out of his or her way to offer it.

———

One of the miracles of leadership is getting even more out of people than they thought they were capable of themselves. There is actually a considerable window here, because most people—and yes, this includes most men—underestimate their capabilities. That creates fertile ground for leadership.

I was consulting with a client who began her session one morning by vilifying one of her associates as overbearing, pompous, and inconsistent. I said, "Stop. Whoa. That's no way to begin. You have to work with this guy, right, so what else do you know about him? What are his strengths?"

She thought for a moment and then said, "I guess he's pretty creative. He's got good strategic vision. He knows his numbers."

"Okay, good. That's the guy you want to deal with. Now, how are you going to do that? You're going to seed the truth. You're going to create a 'listening.' Tell him he's creative and that he has vision. And then that's the guy he'll have to be."

It doesn't always work, of course.

Mark, the man who I expected to be our team photographer and cameraman for the film version of our project, was not demonstrating commitment to his physical training and was not responding to my expectations of teamwork. Because of this gap between my expectations and his reality, we were forced to part ways following our summit of La Plata Peak in September of last year.

There were a number of reasons for this—none of which had to do with his skill level for his expected assignments—but the heart of it was the fact that his expectations for the climb and his contribution to the team were far from mine in terms of preparation and attitude. When you show up for a cold-weather climb to 14,000 feet without a proper coat or boots, and your camera is secured around your neck with a shoelace, there is a serious problem. I have to admit I wish this situation had worked itself out, but the alignment of the team and the overall good of the project were more important than having a half-committed member.

I had no idea, at this point, what I would do, but I knew that I could fix the problem. For the sake of the project, I had to.

———

Leadership requires making unpopular decisions for the highest good of the entire team or organization.

———

In the case of our cameraman, his departure left us with a serious hole in our team, not to mention a missing key component for our film. We filled the void when Vince Ruland—a far superior mountaineer to our departed cameraman—joined our group, and I assumed the role of cameraman-in-waiting. I had no idea how to film a climb, but I was very much in tune with the project and its needs. The one would balance the other. It had to.

———

Even with the departure of Mark and the addition of a new member, I still felt the trajectory of the Aconcagua Man Project was in the state of a healthy, vibrant arc.

———

By this time, the training for our team's January 2011 climb was in full swing and was defined by three distinct approaches.

On Monday evening at five-thirty, we would meet at Red Rocks Amphitheater for training with heavy packs. We began in July with ten-pound packs. Knowing that we would face Aconcagua with fifty-pound packs on our backs, it was Eric's goal that we would be training with full packs by November. And we were.

Tuesday mornings, we would meet again at Red Rocks for anaerobic training. Anaerobic training focuses on drills that are shorter in duration than aerobic training, and usually last less than two minutes. Oxygen is not a limiting factor in this type of training; rather it requires energy from anaerobic sources like phosphagen and lactic acid produced by the climber's body. It was killer stuff, such as running stairs, doing intervals, pounding push-ups, straining over pull-ups, and anything else that Eric could think of to push us a little harder.

Our schedule also included seven 14ers:
1. August 8 - Lincoln Democrat & Bross
2. September 12 - La Plata Peak
3. September 26 - Longs Peak
4. October 29 and 30 - Mayflower Gulch
5. November 20 and 21 – James Peak
6. December 4 – Grizzly Peak
7. January 2, 2011 – Quandary X2 Peak

The latter four of these climbs, Eric deemed as "cold weather" training exercises meant to mimic the snowing and blizzard conditions that were almost inevitable on Aconcagua.

The team also committed to individual workouts of one and a half to two hours, four times a week, carrying fifty pound packs.

Longs Peak proved to be
a turning point for the team.

———

September 26, a beautiful, nearly perfect fall day was marred when we reached the famous Longs Peak Keyhole, as it's called, and were informed by the Forest Service that a man named John Regan had been killed in a fall. We saw his body extracted from the mountain, and the absolute seriousness of what we intended to do on the slopes of Aconcagua hit us all like a ton of bricks.

I can remember standing near Jeff Patterson and watching the helicopter move away with John's body. It was surreal. One moment a man is on the top of the world and the next minute, he is gone. I had a moment with Jeff then that I will never forget. The precious nature of life was right there in my face, and it affected the feelings inside me about our team moving forward. What if one of us died? How would I handle that? All of these men were my friends. I knew their wives and children. Perhaps, I thought at the time, climbing high mountains was not for me after all.

John Regan's wife, Dian, told us later that he had always wanted to climb Aconcagua, and it felt as if we had lost a member of our fraternity. Troy Wagner promised Dian that we would carry John's memory up to the summit with us and would honor him once we got there. Those were not just words. In fact, there was something about that promise that really served as a barometer for what the Aconcagua Man Project truly was all about.

Later, we all talked about this experience and what it meant to us as men. Troy led the charge, using this very sad incident as a vehicle of inspiration for our team and as a way to honor John.

That incident, like any "Aconcagua" endeavor a person pursues, did indeed have the power to inspire. We couldn't let that power go without an authentic response. We had to bring the message of inspiration to the world. Not that what we were doing was more valid than any other endeavor a man or woman embarks upon, but that any time we set our sights on something meaningful and game-changing, we owe it to world to share it.

Men too often fear sharing, as if what they are doing is ordinary or insignificant, when just the opposite is true. If you, as a man, believe without equivocation in the goal you're pursuing, then that belief alone makes it a source of inspiration to others.

Process vs. Purpose

This leads to another consideration that is a sticking point for many men.

"Purpose" is defined by action, by doing, by the heat of battle.

———

**Process is easy for a man; we love to dream.
Purpose is where real growth and change occur:
where satisfaction and fulfillment become reality.**

———

The Aconcagua Man Project's purpose was set by the time we finished our list of 14ers. Our equipment had been purchased. We were getting into the best shape of our lives. Aconcagua was less than a month away. The team was evolving.

9 TIME TO CLIMB

The preparation phase of the Aconcagua Man Project ended with an assortment of meaningful, compelling sub-plots, both business and personal.

We all had lives above and beyond the project. We were all engaged in careers that called for full-time hours. We all had relationships that required our attention and devotion. Professional commitments, ironically, are often harder to put on hold than personal ones, and some of these relationships suffered from a certain amount of inattention, given the rigors of our training. On the other hand, some of these relationships took on new and unexpected dynamics, given our commitment to the project.

Jeff was in a serious relationship with his girlfriend, Lindsay, and their situation was at a crossroads. They had been engaging in conversations regarding the direction of their relationship for some time. Jeff was of two minds about marriage and family. He was also deeply in love. How would the climb impact Jeff and Lindsay?

I was coming out of a three-year relationship with Leslie, a woman I thought I would marry. I was very much in love and living with her and her two boys, Parker and Griffin. In the middle of the Aconcagua project, among many other business and personal commitments, we chose to end our relationship. It was extremely painful for me, and I don't think I really knew how much stress I was feeling. It was more than just moving out of my home. There was also a feeling of being yanked out of my rhythm of relationship in the midst all that was going on. It was challenging, and I hoped I could use it as an opportunity for growth.

Greg was adopting a baby from Russia. His wife Laura was pregnant. In addition, he was maintaining a heavy travel schedule and was up for a significant promotion to the executive level at IHG. The pre-climb holidays, normally a time for family, instead included the uncomfortable task of explaining how and why he would shortly be taking leave of his growing brood to spend three weeks in Argentina. His father-in-law pulled him aside for a private chat during one of these Christmas celebrations and very candidly said, "Your Aconcagua isn't a mountain in Argentina, Greg. It's a family here in Colorado." How would Greg deal with that perspective?

Eric's marriage was at a turning point. His wife, Adina, older by a few years and more established in her career, was ready to start a family. Two weeks before boarding a plane for Mendoza, Eric didn't know where this dilemma was going to take him. He had just started a new business, and all of his energy was focused there. Leaving for three weeks to follow a dream was bound to affect both of these situations. Would the affect be positive or negative?

Vince was in the midst of a divorce. He had two daughters who were going through the turmoil that all kids experience when they are in the middle of a domestic dispute. He was also the project leader for a highly important satellite program and managing upwards of fifty other employees. Leaving for Argentina for three weeks was cause for all kinds of negotiations, but it was also cause for enough emotional turmoil that I had to wonder how the pendulum would swing for Vince during the climb. In truth, Vince had very little quality time with the team, and a part of me wondered if he would fit in.

Dennis was a study in determination. He had prepared as hard as anyone for the climb and his family was behind him one hundred percent, but he was leaving at a time when the real estate business was bad. At sixty-seven, he was undertaking one of the most physically demanding endeavors he'd ever faced. He was being pulled in a number of directions, and I was eager to see what kind of answers Dennis would get from the climb. He had so much going on. He even had his computer turned on at the airport in Denver and went so far as to find wireless access in Santiago before we shuttled over to Mendoza. If his focus on that computer was any indication of the focus he would bring to the mountain, he would most certainly be on the summit.

Troy, in his mid-thirties and also coming out of a life-changing divorce, was a man in search of an identity both from a career standpoint and in his view of personal relationships in general. The climb would take him far away from both, and I could foresee an extraordinary growth opportunity for Troy. Would Troy embrace the learning he had experienced on James Peak with the same vigor on Aconcagua? What would happen going forward for this man, as he tested himself at a very cellular level?

Once you move an "Aconcagua" endeavor from the preparation stage to the battlefield, a good amount of your energy goes into making use of the tactics you've designed in support of your strategy. It's not, by any means, that the long view is forgotten, but once the door opens on your new restaurant or you've accepted a new position with a firm, you now have to make good on the climb. That requires tremendous focus, patience, and consistent behavior.

**You put one foot in front of the other.
You take care of the next thing
on your list of immediate needs.**

All of our conversation about service and creating a better world would take a backseat to accomplishing the summit. Service and creating a better world would have to wait for the integration stage of the project.

What we could not forget, however, was that the impact of the climb itself would dictate how we approached integration once we returned home.

We couldn't predict the impact of the climb, but we could safely say that the preparation phase of the project had been successful.

For some of us, including me, it was often easy to forget the importance of acknowledging this phase. When I stop for a moment and reflect back, I can say that this part of the project was kick-in-the-ass fun. So as you discover your personal "Aconcagua," make certain you enjoy the preparation phase and stop long enough to praise your progress. After all, you don't really know what will happen next. But now, it was time to climb.

PART II – THE CLIMB

10 PATIENCE AND VULNERABILITY

Like every venture of any consequence or note, the Aconcagua Man Project was a three-part endeavor: the preparation, the climb, and the integration.

We talked about the Preparation in Part I. It begins with a conscious decision to find out what it is that you want and what you are willing to do to have it. The next phase begins with the actual event: the putting of the boots on the ground. Game on.

Part II is the Climb. For us, it began when we boarded a plan in Denver and endured twenty-two hours of travel time—much of it hampered by unexpected delays—and landed with high hopes in Santiago, Chile. A quick turnaround was not to be; here we faced the potential of a pending airline strike and union unrest and another nine-hour layover. It would have been easy for any one of us to suffer a meltdown of some type or another, and it probably would have been justified. Instead, we feasted on chocolate, coffee, and good humor. We read, dozed, and waited.

It was in the Santiago airport that I met a Brazilian marathon runner—an extremely fit-looking man—who was also on his way to Aconcagua. This was his fourth attempt? He had yet to summit. He was trying again.

———

Five thousand people each year make the trek to Mendoza with every intention of climbing the 22,834 feet to the great mountain's summit, and only fifteen hundred make it. That's thirty percent; not a great ratio.

———

It could very well be that many of these people are unprepared for the realities of such a climb, but the numbers nonetheless speak for themselves. I felt grateful that I had hooked up with Rodrigo from Aventuras Patagonicas (AP) to take our team up the mountain. AP has the highest success rate on the mountain and a strong penchant for safety. I wanted the Aconcagua Man Project to have the best shot at a summit bid, and I also think this speaks to life in general. Failure is a reality. Half of all businesses fail within four years. But in most cases, these are the same people who pick themselves up, dust themselves off, and jump back into the game.

We didn't travel to Argentina thinking that anything less than the summit of Aconcagua would signal a successful venture. We'd already succeeded in so many ways. We'd set a goal: to use the Aconcagua project as a way of growing and changing, as a way of becoming more effective leaders, and as a way of discovering more about ourselves as men.

Did we all picture ourselves on the summit? I certainly did. But so did that marathon runner I mentioned. Were my teammates equally committed? Nobody really knows what is in the heart of another man, unless, of course, he shows you.

After nine frustrating hours, we boarded a plane for Mendoza, climbing high above the Andes, with the great Aconcagua looming in the background. And yes, the power in the airport in Mendoza was on the fritz when we got there. It was another hour before we could deplane. Well, at this point, what was another hour?

The Climb, as we will see later in the book, leads to the Part III of any venture, and that is the integration of what we have learned and experienced—including the missteps and the failures—into the continuing journey we call our lives. Without this integration, we cannot turn transformation into evolution. And if we don't do that, then all our efforts in the preparation and climbing stages are left in limbo.

It's probably good to state up front that the Climb, whether we're talking about the great mountain of Aconcagua or our personal "inner" Aconcagua, is not a finite endeavor. It truly is infinite. It doesn't begin one day and end somewhere down the road. That's not how an evolution of mind, body, and spirit happens. The Climb is that journey toward learning and mastery that never really ends, but which always keeps our chosen purpose in sight.

That purpose was best demonstrated by us in challenging the mighty slopes of Aconcagua for sixteen days and by the simple act of putting one foot in front of the other. For us, it was a commitment to the process and a willingness to fight through violent headaches, shortness of breath, and the sheer punishment of traveling forty-five-plus miles on foot in rarified air where the risk of pulmonary or cerebral edema was something we lived with every day.

Patience: that was the lesson of the day. Spirit had already gifted us with thirty hours of arduous travel from Denver to Mendoza. It was a good lesson.

As eager as we were to get started, we realized that once we got on the mountain, patience would be one of our most important allies.

We checked into the Park Hyatt Hotel. This was a very nice hotel that would be our last taste of western living for twenty-three days. The plan was to spend two days in Mendoza. I felt it was important to acclimate ourselves to our surroundings, to get acquainted with our guides, and to put our equipment in order.

We had dinner with our guide team the first night and feasted on steaks and seafood and consumed copious amounts of the local Malbec. We called our local guides Gusto and Rolo, and they were clearly masters of the mountain.

I can only describe Augusto as a deep man. Now in his early fifties, he had been climbing mountains since he was fourteen and had made the summit of Aconcagua fifty-six times: an insurmountable world record if ever there was one. Gusto was a sage. He moved through the streets of Mendoza as if the mountains were in his blood, melding speed and alacrity with an unmatched gracefulness. When I asked him about Aconcagua, he answered by saying, "Mountains are not dangerous. The problem lies with the people who climb dangerously."

Rolo, the younger of the two, was quiet and perceptive. He was a Mendoza native, and his English was passable at best. I could tell right from the beginning that there was a sweet strength about this man, especially when he was reminiscing about his wife and three "Niños." His home and the mountains were clearly Rolo's first loves, and I was already looking forward to spending more time with him.

Our head guide was Mike Bradley. He was a resident of Vail, Colorado and a veteran of twelve seasons on the slopes of Aconcagua, with eighteen summits under his belt. Mike impressed me right from the beginning as a man of action, with rock solid integrity and competence. Over dinner, he regaled us with countless stories about the great mountain, and we were all transfixed and inspired. Mike didn't pull any punches as he talked about the dangers confronting us. He didn't withhold anything as he described the winds and the sub-zero weather. Over dinner that first night, he set the tone by telling us that his last expedition had been the very worst of his career. Oh, great.

He described what is called the "High Camp," an open-face section of the mountain where gale-force winds can literally pummel you for hours. He and several clients he was guiding nearly died on the mountain; they had quite literally been blown off it. Mike had been forced to lead a retreat in the middle of the night.

I liked Mike's style. He gave us the worst-case scenario. Then he went on to describe, in equally vivid terms, the wonders we were about to experience and the thrills we were about to encounter.

———

I could tell that Mike's impression of our team was positive. There was an air of relaxation that was unmistakable.

———

We were ready. We were confident. We were well-equipped. Gregarious Greg with his humor and his positive energy; Jeff with an extraordinary talent for engagement and insight; Troy with his steady, consistent, and quiet strength; Dennis with his statesman-like aura; Vince with the quiet confidence of a mountaineer extraordinaire ;Eric with a sense of youthful wisdom.

I found myself grateful beyond words. There was a spirit that bound us together. This was a group ready to embrace the Climb.

But two days, as it turned out, was too much to spend in Mendoza. We'd come to climb a mountain. We spent two days wishing we were doing so.

The morning of the third day, we packed our gear into the two vans that would take us west from Mendoza to Penitentes, a ski area resting at an elevation of 8,500 feet. It's a drive that winds along the Rio Mendoza deep into the heart of the rugged Andes Mountains. We drove for two hours, gaining altitude continually. We were all in good spirits. If there was a tendril of anxiety running through the group, it was not much different than the launch of any endeavor long in the planning.

.

People don't like the word "anxiety."
I say, get over it.
Being anxious is not a bad thing. It's energy.
It tells you you're doing something laced with
uncomfortable feelings, and that's a good thing.

Remember: move from certainty to uncertainty. If you don't have some anxiety in your life, then you're running scared from all that life has to offer. You don't want to be that guy.

Our team began our acclimatization in Penitentes, where we were only 3,000 feet higher than Denver, but resting a night there set the tempo for the rest of the climb.

Tempo and acclimatization: they sound like hiking terms, but sometimes men don't recognize the need to pace themselves. Some people think that pacing yourself means you're loafing or getting your ass kicked by someone else. Actually, it doesn't.

Yes, sometimes we want to jump in with both feet and a shortage of foresight. But here's the thing. Writing a book is a page-at-a-time proposition. Building a business takes years. Becoming a successful business consultant is years in the making. Ignoring tempo and the need to adjust can be a killer, and not just on a mountain at altitude.

Women say they want their guys to be cautious and
watchful. I don't buy it.

**I think women are attracted to guys who try new
things, love life, and give their deepest gifts to
humanity every single day.**

———

So here we were, in Penitentes. The accommodations
were, in a word, rustic; it proved to be much closer to a
hostel than a hotel. The food sucked. The beds squeaked. It
was the best we would see for weeks, and the general
attitude of the guys was: Let's get moving.

That afternoon, we all took some time to explore. It
was rugged country: high desert, very rocky, and beautiful
in an austere, compelling way. One thing was clear. This
wasn't the high Rockies where pine trees and aspen are
plentiful. We'd see no trees from here on out.

I'd like to say that I slept like a baby that one night in
Penitentes, but it was actually the restless sleep of a man
getting ready to set out on an adventure into the
unexpected. I woke up refreshed.

———

**The route our guides had planned for us was called
the Ameghino Valley Upper Guanacos Traverse.**

———

The first stage was a three-day hike up the Vacas and
Ameghino Valleys to Base Camp. We had the luxury of
pack mules on this first stage, which was good, because
we'd be traveling forty miles over three days and gaining
5,300 feet in altitude.

We drove twenty minutes to the trailhead and the
gateway to the park. There was a stone shack, and two
park rangers with the singular job of checking your papers

and making sure you'd paid the $750-per-person entrance fee.

We were excited, as you can well imagine. We'd been waiting for four days. It was time to put the boots on the trail, as the saying goes. The mules were packed, and we were making final preparations with our daypacks—water, snack bars, and rain gear—when Mike Bradley, our lead guide, approached us with a troubled look on his face. I knew something was up. He looked like a man with the weight of the world on his shoulders.

"I need to talk to you guys," he said. We all gathered around. A ripple of unease moved from man to man. Mike suddenly broke down. I could see tears welling up in his eyes. What the heck was going on? "My girlfriend broke up with me last night. We were on the phone and…"

He couldn't hold back the tears. He shoulders shook, and he began to cry. "I didn't see it coming. I thought we'd…"

Oh, man. Could her timing have been any worse? Here was our guide, ten minutes away from leading us into the waiting arms of an unrelenting monster, and now he was dealing with this. How would we seven guys, expecting the best out of the man in charge of a quest nearly nine months in the making, react? It could have gone any number of ways, but it was Greg who stepped forward and put a reassuring arm around Mike's shoulder. What he essentially said was, "Whatever you need, we're here, Mike."

That was exactly how it went, one team member after another offering support and empathy. A pat on the back, a well-meaning word, a giant bear hug. Mike was part of our team, but he was also a guy dealing with all the extraneous, unavoidable trappings of daily life. Boots on the trail could wait for a few minutes.

**That's how it is. Life doesn't stop
just because you're at the doorstep of a great
mountain, a critical business decision,
or a seminal experience.**

Mike was amazing in that moment. He was open and vulnerable. Many men would not have opened up like that. And I can tell you that it was exactly what was needed at the time. He is a strong man; in this very vulnerable moment, he became stronger. We grew as a team in that moment as well, but that was only the first of many surprises we would experience over the days to come.

"I'll get it together," Mike promised. "I might need a little space for a few hours, but we've got a big day ahead of us, and I'm glad you guys are with me."

Our team had grown stronger in light of what had happened, not weaker or divided. The type of collaborative leadership demonstrated in that moment proved to be a powerful learning experience. I would take it back with me when I returned home, and I would put it to good use in my practice.

**Vulnerability is a powerful tool.
It binds people together.
It creates a common perspective.
Vulnerability can actually be empowering.**

When we set out a few minutes later, it was not with heavy hearts. Mike was one of us now. He had some things to work through, to be sure, and we would be there for him if he needed us. In the meantime, Aconcagua called.

It was warm in the high desert at 8,500 feet. Some of us were even wearing hiking shorts. Hats, sunglasses, and sunscreen would soon become our best friends, because the sun was cutting at this altitude.

This route was not as heavily traveled as the other options up the mountain, and this fit our team's style. The "road less traveled" may sound like a cliché, but it's almost always the more satisfying way to go.

Gusto told us that this particular route up Aconcagua was first established by a Polish Expedition in 1934, and it tread over high desert slopes that burst with subtle shades of greens and browns, dominated by fields of sage. The mountains of the high ranges slipped into view in the distance, and their jagged peaks were heavy with snow and looked spectacular. The sun felt good on our backs.

By mid-afternoon, we had left whatever foliage the mountains had to offer behind us.

Many people call Aconcagua the Rock Pile. And for good reason, I suppose. A day into the hike, there are no trees—not one—and little vegetation. Some people view the mountain ranges of the Andes and the road to Aconcagua as boring, stark, and unimaginative. For people like this, the challenge, I imagine, is scaling the barren slopes and traversing the vast rock fields with the singular goal of reaching the summit.

The discerning eye sees so much more on the slopes and valleys leading to Aconcagua. A palette of silvers, grays, and blues, dashed with purples, blacks, and the most brilliant whites imaginable. Contours of stone, snow, and

117

ice that come together to form a canvas of multi-dimensions that seem to change moment to moment, that absorb the blues of the sky and the blushing grays and whites of the clouds like a wash of watercolor, and tempt your imagination to see a landscape unique to this one place on earth.

———

**Beauty is something you see with your eyes,
but you really experience it
with your heart and your soul.**

———

We walked for seven hours that first day, covered fifteen miles, and gained 2,000 feet in altitude. Welcome to the Andes. The energy level was good. The conversation was typical guy stuff. The laughter was spirited. We were accustomed to these altitudes, and we all felt strong on this day.

The real work was ahead of us. The suffering was yet to come.

The three-day climb to base camp gave us a chance to reacquaint ourselves with our tents and our overnight gear, and to enjoy two nights of relatively ambient weather. We discovered rock basketball, care of Greg Aden's exemplary imagination. First, you make a basket on the ground with rocks. Then gather up a good stash of fist-sized rocks—and there was no shortage of these. Then find a comfortable spot to sit back and start shooting. Our team was reputed to have more energy at the end of the day than any other team these guides had been with. Our training had paid off, at least for now. We were ready to drink some Yerba Mate, eat, and recover from a full day of hiking.

The second day on the mountain was much like the first: long and hot. It took us through the Vacas Valley. We had no shortage of positive energy, and a new-found comfort level with the surroundings. It was interesting, though, as we climbed higher and got deeper into the expedition, I could feel each individual on the team focusing more. We talked less; we upped our concentration.

Every afternoon on this mountain there is strong weather. The clouds roll in. The wind kicks up. You hear thunder. The showers are welcome after the hot sun, but when you understand that the storms you are getting here are merely the last remnants of much more severe weather further up, the reality of what lies ahead becomes more apparent.

Later at night, when the clouds part, the stars explode across the sky: a light show like nothing any of us has ever seen before. Where did they all come from? Eric and I stood outside our tents that night completely mesmerized, and I swear the air hummed with the power raining down on us. I felt humble. Maybe that's the best thing about Mother Nature. She brings perspective to our lives and reminds us that our part in the universe is miniscule. It's up to us to make it meaningful. As human beings, we tend to look at ourselves as the most important things in the universe. Standing on the deserted slopes of the Andes, with a million stars radiating from the cosmos, makes you realize that the only "universe" you can truly affect is the one you live in; you can touch people or you can isolate yourself; you can bring your best gifts to the table and share them with the world, or you can settle for an insignificant legacy.

I went to bed that night feeling inspired. I also felt a moment of anxiety. I could feel my body working to adjust to the altitude, but it was nothing too uncomfortable. Troy was becoming strangely quiet and more pensive. Jeff and Greg offered comedic relief. Dennis was a focused machine. The guides, including Mike, were doing fine. I had a good conversation with Mike about his break-up. I could tell he was hurting, but I could also tell he was still as solid as the mountain we were climbing. It was brisk the following morning, even chilly. The third day led us into the Ameghino Valley, a wide stretch of rocky terrain rising ever higher toward the west. The highlight of that day was a mandatory crossing of the Ameghino River. It's not a particularly deep body of water, but it's deep enough and frigid enough that we had to ride the mules across, one man at a time.

It was a good time for cleaning up, and one of the last spots on the trail. Privacy? Not a problem. We were not alone on Aconcagua, but the people were truly few and far between.

Once the river was navigated, we ate fruit and sandwiches and set out again. We paced ourselves. A series of switchbacks led us higher into the mountains and gave us a taste of things to come. Mike Bradley took photographs of the team and expanding panorama. I ran my Go Pro; a small, wearable, high-definition camera.

———

**We finally glimpsed the towering peaks
of the great mountain and its snowcapped
companions in the distance,
and wonder and awe took over.**

———

120

As eager as we were to reach Base Camp, where the real odyssey would begin, back-to-back-to-back days of hiking for seven-hour stretches cannot be minimized. Base Camp was located in a carved-out bowl at 13,800 feet, an altitude where few people ever go, even those of us who live in Colorado with fifty-four 14ers in our backyard. We had climbed 5,300 feet in three days, and the real work, without mules, had yet to begin.

Base Camp is a fairly permanent facility. It is set in a field of dirt and stone dotted with at least twenty large, very colorful, tent-like structures assigned to each of the guide companies. This flat, desolate sweep of living space is surrounded by rounded hills that radiate a rose-colored tint when the light is just right. It's oddly appealing to my personal aesthetic, but then I can find beauty in almost any natural setting.

There were a hundred or so other people camping there that night. Each guiding company had its own area. Aventuras Patagonicas' area had a permanent mess tent large enough to service our entire team with room to spare. The company employed two full-time employees at Base Camp, and they did a good job of pampering us. No one complained.

We spent a full rest day at Base Camp. The word "rest" was crucial in this description, because we had covered forty miles in three days, but also because we needed the time for the process of acclimatization. The definition is simple: altitude acclimatization is the process of adjusting to decreasing oxygen levels at higher elevations. More to the point is needing to do everything possible to avoid altitude sickness. At its worst, acute altitude sickness can progress to pulmonary edema or cerebral edema. They can both get you a ticket down the mountain. And if not treated, they can be potentially fatal.

———

The trek to the summit of Aconcagua was not a sprint. We were going to go slowly and allow our bodies time to acclimate. This is the single most important strategy for success at high altitudes.

———

Like any individual or organizational goal, planning is of extreme importance. The best leaders recognize the power of sustainability. As a leader, you communicate your purpose, provide inspiration, and offer direction.

Our sixteen days on Aconcagua were no different. We needed to trust the strategy and implement the tactics. And sometimes the best tactic is to take a step back and gather yourself together for the next assault. That's what our rest day was all about.

11 THE ART OF ACCLIMATIZATION

"No new behavior shows up on the mountain."

This is a belief that comes from years of conducting leadership seminars. I used to say to the participants in these sessions that a three-day seminar was not a place to expect new behaviors. If you're a passive person in the seminar, it is reflective of your having a passive personality out in the real world. If you're gregarious, flighty, or intense in the seminar, it's a safe bet that you're the same way in the workplace and at home. This was neither a criticism nor a compliment, only an observation.

The question I always asked was, "If your behavior in the work place is hindering your ability to be successful or to lead, then you'll only change it by a full awareness of the problem or by finding an effective way to use the behavior to your benefit. Owning it is the first step."

———

My observations of the team during those first three days were fascinating, especially in retrospect.

———

Eric was strong, positive, and relentless; nothing less than reaching the summit ever entered his mind, but he was the kind of man who worried as much about the guys he had trained as he did about himself. Would he sacrifice himself for the team?

Vince was fitting into a group that had been together for months, but he was also a mountaineer, first and foremost. He understood that the summit of a mountain was only a step in the process, that it was a goal, but only one of many goals. Would he be satisfied with something less than Aconcagua's summit?

Dennis was a total inspiration. I often followed in his footprints, as the saying goes about the man in front of you. He also made more than one reference to High Camp being a respectable goal in his mind, and High Camp was 3,000 feet from the summit.

Jeff was hurting almost from the beginning; struggling with headaches and nausea that he made little mention of to anyone, save me, his tent mate. He just kept going. His fitness was high, but he was not the athlete that Eric was or the mountaineer that Vince was. How would he do higher up?

Troy was like a machine, though there was a stoicism that made me concerned about his mindset. He had kept the lowest profile since we left Denver, and we would need the leadership of each member as we climbed higher. Would he share himself with the team and communicate his needs?

Greg laughed, joked, and took the lead in keeping the group loose. Greg had missed considerable training time back home, and I hoped it wouldn't affect him now. He had left a new family behind in Denver, and that was also at the forefront of his mind, after the advice his father-in-law had given him. How would that affect him?

———

I had my own issues.

———

I had arrived on the mountain with an ongoing case of plantar fasciitis, which is an irritation and swelling of the thick tissue on the bottom of the foot that is very uncomfortable. I didn't really speak about it with the team, but I had to wonder if that would affect me going forward.

Then we met with the park doctor just before embarking at the trailhead. This was routine. They didn't want people with debilitating problems attempting to conquer the high altitude conditions of Aconcagua, which was very considerate of them. I didn't anticipate any problem with any of the guys, and certainly not with me.

They checked my lungs: perfect.

They checked my blood oxygen level: 96. Which was amazing, given the fact that we were already two miles above sea level.

———

Then they checked my blood pressure.
It registered an alarming 160/80.

———

Wait. What? That was impossible. My normal blood pressure at home was 110/60, an exceptionally healthy level for a man my age. But my grandfather had died from a heart attack that was likely caused by high blood

125

pressure some years back, and my mind immediately started scaring me.

"It's too high," the doctor told me in broken English. "It's a risk going any further."

Two very obvious statements, but my questions ran a lot deeper than that. "How did this happen? What could have caused it?"

I would be lying if I said this unexpected discovery wasn't on my mind during the three days and the twenty-plus hours we spent forging the valleys to Base Camp. The news was unexpected and disconcerting, but it had to be dealt with.

Sound familiar?

How often do we, as leaders, bump into challenges that are unexpected?

How many times will you run headlong into an obstacle as you summit your own Aconcagua?

Look at our guide, Mike Bradley. Consider the bombshell that he had to deal with when his girlfriend unexpectedly terminated their relationship, via phone, from 3,000 miles away and with zero warning. This was no glancing blow; this was his future changing before his very eyes. And yet, he had a job to do. He had responsibilities that required his full attention. I was amazed by how quickly he responded.

I think this is when we become tempered as leaders. We use trials and tribulations to strengthen us as men and women.

Look at Dennis, a respected and successful real estate developer whose business was torpedoed by a housing and banking crisis that changed the complexion of his industry forever. He, and others like him, have had to let go of an old model and create a new one in order to thrive. In

Dennis's case, he cut costs and turned to managing the assets that he had.

This is life.

———

As a leadership consultant, I am constantly correcting my own course and assisting others in adjusting their current trajectory.

———

When I arrived at Base Camp, the doctor found that my blood pressure had risen to 180/80. Incredulous, I was also seriously concerned now. What the hell was going on? Our guide presented the doctor with all of my medical records, but the doctor was not impressed. He gave me two options. "You can take the blood pressure medicine that we prescribe, or you can turn around and return to Mendoza. Your choice."

Nine months of planning. Nine months of intense training. I was in the best shape of my life. Now what? Some adjustments are minor. Some are major.

"Do I quit?" I asked Troy a few minutes later.

Internally, my thoughts were even deeper. "If I continue, am I going to die?" I was terrified. I let my mind go to the dark side.

It was a very real consideration. We had another 9,000 feet to climb, and I had no clue why this was happening to me, or what my body was trying to tell me.

This atmosphere of uncertainty and fear is what I call the "silent killer."

We all know about fear. Fear is the emotional response we have to a perceived threat. It is the most basic survival instinct. It very often kicks in whether there is a

127

specific stimulus to trigger it or not. Pain triggers it. The possibility of danger triggers it. Uncertainty definitely triggers it.

_____

The silent killer is that thing that paralyzes us from taking action that we know can change our lives.

_____

I cannot tell you how many guys that I talked with after sending out invitations who were enthralled by the idea of the Aconcagua Man Project. I can't tell you how often I saw a guy's eyes light up, like a child on Christmas morning, just hearing me describe the program and the plan. I can't tell you how often I heard the yearning in their voice as they debated the commitment.

It was just too big for some men to fathom; I anticipated that. It just didn't appeal to others. I got that too. But there were many among those who turned down the invitation because of the silent killer. They could almost taste the power of the commitment and the rush of the adrenaline. But fear and uncertainty hung over their heads like a mother's cautionary word keeping them from exploring just beyond the fence of the backyard. They clearly wanted it. They just couldn't make the leap. It was too paralyzing.

I had that moment in Base Camp. I faced a decision. Would the silent killer win out? It was a very valid question.

I don't like the idea of taking prescription medicines. They are a last resort. But I had come this far. I didn't want my journey to end ignominiously, though not everyone would view it that way. It was decision time. I had twenty minutes to make a decision to stay or to go. In the end, I agreed to take the blood pressure medicine, though even that was a source of anxiety. I had no idea how my body might react to it.

Vince confided in me that he had been taking a similar medication since his doctor had found a problem with his blood pressure prior to the trip. There was some consolation in that. It's like hearing someone in your own industry reveal an obstacle similar to one you might be facing. It helps to know that someone has made similar adjustments in combating that roadblock. But no two roadblocks are alike, no matter how similar. Of course, later I found out from Mike Bradley that having a high blood pressure reading at altitude can quite simply be the body's way of "adjusting" to a higher elevation. Whatever the cause, it gave me reason to speculate on my own mental assuredness.

———

My high blood pressure reading was a good test for my mental and emotional commitment to the climb.

———

I'm glad to report that I didn't quit the climb. The situation did lead to one of the more interesting and revealing aspects of the first three days of our journey, in particular when you couple it with the many hours of travel and delays we had endured in getting to our destination. I'm talking about group dynamics: a subject particularly germane to our discussion about adaptations.

Personalities clash. Stress invokes confrontation. Men get on each other's nerves just as women get on each other's nerves. Group settings can either bring out the best in people or the worst.

We had powerful and diverse personalities on our team. We had all been adjusting to each other, learning about each other, and, through it all, creating a powerful leadership culture on the team.

The first three days of our journey set the stage. We didn't have one altercation or disagreement. I expected a couple of, "Do that again, and I'll kick your ass," comments, but they didn't happen. We did have an "asshole of the day" award. Dennis gave the first of these to Troy, when he inadvertently did something to piss off Dennis. I will never forget the tone in Dennis's voice when he looked at Troy and declared, "You're just an asshole."

Yet, even with the "asshole of the day" award, the team held together. Respect won out. My goal for a collaborative leadership experience began to coalesce.

"Do that again, and I'll kick your ass," or some form of that, is a workplace phenomenon. Sure, the "kick your ass" part might be a metaphor for one-upmanship or backstabbing, but it happens every day in almost every business.

I see it in my work as a leadership consultant all the time as I try to bring elements of collaboration to a dysfunctional corporate team. What you quickly discover is that the difference between a team being aligned and one that is at odds within itself is the difference between a company going bankrupt and one earning huge profits. On a mountain, it can mean the difference between life and death, as we all learned during our infamous training climb on James Peak.

**The difference between team agreement
and alignment is the difference
between life and death on a mountain.**

How does a great leader get the most out of his people? How do you invoke collaboration on a team?

First, you make sure everyone understands the purpose of your Aconcagua.

Then, you bring an understanding to that purpose, though that understanding may well be different for every person and require a different level of communication. Together, you create a direction that makes sense of your purpose and gives people the tools they will need to be able to accomplish the end result.

Finally, you make people accountable for their actions, but you also give them a sense of ownership in the outcome.

**Everyone wants to be a person of action.
Really, they do.
Everyone wants to get his or her hands dirty:
figuratively, if not literally.
A true leader gives them the chance.**

A true leader is also fully in tune with the art of adaptation that we have been discussing, and day six since our arrival in the Argentina was just that: a day of adjustment.

131

Our guides from Aventuras Patagonicas called this day at Base Camp a day of rest and acclimatization. It was an extremely wise decision, because they wanted what the Aconcagua team wanted: the best possible chance for the seven of us to make the summit. The most effective way to accomplish this goal was to take the time necessary for our bodies to acclimatize to the low oxygen environment. The idea throughout our trek would be to incorporate rest days into our schedule and to climb in "traditional expedition style."

Why take this approach, as opposed to a more straightforward, get-your-ass-up-the-mountain-as-fast-as-humanly-possible approach? Isn't that why we had trained as hard as we did for months on end? Weren't we here to reinforce our purpose as men? Wasn't this our chance to go head-to-head with the elements and measure our strength and courage accordingly?

The answer was simple. There was nothing macho about risking life and limb in the name of arrogance and foolishness. That behavior is not to be mistaken for risk. Risk has its place. Getting out of bed in the morning comes with a certain number of inherent risks. Trekking a mountain like Aconcagua has inherent risks too, and an effective leader plans for these risks. He or she looks forward to them. Strength and courage are worthy virtues that have nothing to do with poor planning. If you fail because of poor planning, you've demonstrated neither courage nor strength, and you certainly haven't shown the qualities of a good leader.

A good leader works with the best people he or she can find. Our guides—Mike, Gusto, and Rolo—were as good as they come, which was why I hired them. Their decision to exploit a traditional expedition style produced results, and that's all a good leader cares about: results.

What this style entailed was a series of "carry" days. On those days, we would carry loads up to the next camp further up the mountain and then return to eat and sleep once again at the previous camp. This was our opportunity to move the majority of our gear to the next camp, cache it there, and then drop back to the lower altitude of the previous camp.

The day following a carry day was a "move" day, where we moved what remained of our stuff to the higher camp. This is considered by most in the field to be the best method of acclimatization. It was one reason why Aventuras Patagonicas had such an exemplary record for successful summits: their schedules of rest, acclimate, and climb.

There is a Zen quality to this approach that allows you to enjoy the endeavor more fully, and it applies to any "Aconcagua" endeavor.

The rest day at Base Camp allowed the team to recover from three days of serious hiking of over forty miles and going up nearly 6,000 feet in altitude change.

———

**My friend Terry Tillman would often say,
"The pauses are just as important as the action,"
and in climbing Aconcagua,
this was proven to be a true statement.**

———

Men often don't recognize the value of taking a step back to evaluate where they've been, what they've learned along the way, and how they can apply those lessons going forward.

This shortcoming takes a toll both personally and professionally. I know. I've been affected by impatience for a good part of my life.

Relationships, for one thing, are always works in progress, and some of us want them to work without the growing pains. But the growing pains are what make relationships more vibrant and special. When you make strides in a relationship, you build a foundation with long-term potential. You discover a person's strengths and come to respect them, but you also learn about a person's shortcomings and learn to accept them.

There are two behaviors that men often use to avoid the growing pains: they stomp away and slam the door behind them or they throw up their hands in surrender. It's probably safe to say that neither approach has a chance in hell of manifesting growth or change. We've been talking about evolution and transformation. Both require a healthy dose of self-honesty, and when you enter any relationship from a position of self-honesty, you welcome the growth that comes with it.

Stomping away and slamming the door only serves to exacerbate the situation. That's pretty obvious. You've put off finding a resolution to the situation, and you've disrespected both yourself and the other person involved. All you've managed to do is create a bigger mess and more unresolved issues.

Surrender is just as debilitating because men often mistake acquiescence with concrete progress. Saying "Yes, dear," doesn't add strength to a relationship. It may gloss over a disagreement, but, in essence, it never solves a thing. Saying "Yes, dear," becomes a habit that makes you soft, and we've already established that men in our society are getting softer by the minute. Suddenly, you're seeking approval in all the wrong places instead of steering your own ship in a meaningful direction.

Ralph Waldo Emerson wrote an incredible essay on the subject of self-reliance. His essay speaks to the issue of appeasing others to achieve a short-term solution. In the end, we only erode our own self-esteem. I am not saying that men should be unkind to their partners. I am saying be real, be honest, and be authentic and vulnerable. There is much more juice in those areas. It's the same in the business world. Steamrolling your way through the workplace rarely pays dividends. Yes, there are times when you have to kick some butt—it could be anything from a delinquent supplier to a lazy employee—and sometimes the best leadership technique is to heartily confront someone, but usually it's not. In the long run, conversation generally bears more fruit, and listening during a conversation requires a certain degree of patience.

―――

An effective leader understands the art of adaptation. Knowing when to step back is as important as knowing when to take center stage.

―――

As it related to the Aconcagua Man Project, knowing when to trust our guides and the plan they had perfected for getting their charges to the summit showed good leadership. Now it was time for the Aconcagua team to step back and let Mike, Gusto, and Rolo do their jobs.

So we rested. We refueled our bodies. We allowed them to acclimate. We looked ahead, even as we appraised where we had been. We talked, but most of our conversations were about the climb and about the next steps in the process.

During the preparation phase of the project, there was always a thread of conversation that touched upon our long-term goals as men. That was part of the working model that I had intentionally introduced. What do we want as men? What were we willing to do to get there? How could we push the boundaries that our day-to-day lives had created for us? How could we use the discipline we were showing to become better leaders?

Here on the mountain, it wasn't all that different.

———

Our focus was on the climb, but it wasn't meant as an escape from our day-to-day lives. It was meant to give us a new, and hopefully inspired, view of our lives back home.

———

So as we prepared for the next phase of our climb, the experiences of the first phase began to pay dividends. We had begun to acclimatize.

12 HEADACHES AND HIGH CAMP I

Jeff Patterson had the worst of it early on.

He reached Base Camp and felt as if someone had hit him in the head with a baseball bat. The pain was excruciating. Sitting in a chair, aching from head to foot, it hurt him to make eye contact with another person. He could hardly rise from a chair. Making the fifty-foot trek to the outhouse proved to be a monumental task.

Much like my lingering blood pressure issue, Jeff was bombarded by an endless bout of self-doubt and hypercritical questions; the silent killer was preying on another victim. I had asked the same questions: "What is happening to me? We've just started." "What's wrong with me? I thought I was in better shape than this." Jeff shared the same self-doubts I'd been struggling with: "There's absolutely no way I can possibly climb another 9,000 feeling like this."

Of course, he shared none of this with anyone in our team that first evening, even when we gathered for dinner in the Aventuras Patagonicas' mess tent. What would Jeff say to the team, if anything?

―――

We had just begun, and here was a guy falling apart before the real work had even started.

―――

Jeff and I shared a tent that first night in Base Camp, and he finally allowed himself to share some of his anguish. "I feel like a five-year-old," he confessed. You can say that sort of thing to a guy you trust, and Jeff and I had a mutual respect for each other with a long history. "All I want to do is curl up in a ball and cry. I'll never make it to the top feeling like this."

Unfortunately, the rest day didn't help Jeff very much. He still felt the classic symptoms of altitude sickness, only more so. One of the major problems with the kind of headaches and nausea that he was experiencing was a lack of appetite; he didn't want to eat and it was almost impossible to drink, but fueling his body and getting hydrated were essential.

That's what a rest day is primarily for: a day for sleeping and eating. You read some, you commiserate some, and you meditate some. But mostly you sleep, eat, and hydrate. Jeff was having trouble with all three.

That day, we posted this on our web site, under the heading: *Base Camp Is Reached.*

It read:

> *The Aconcagua Team reached Base Camp yesterday.*
>
> *In their first three days, they have covered a distance of thirty miles and have ascended 3,200 feet vertically. Yesterday, they covered thirteen miles to*

138

reach base camp. They currently are at an elevation of 13,000 feet.

Stephen said that Aconcagua is directly in front of them, and it is more majestic and beautiful than they ever could have imagined. Everyone is healthy and in good shape. Some of them did have slight headaches at the end of the day. They managed to get their tents set up just before a snow storm blew in.

Today is a rest day. Tomorrow they will carry loads to an elevation of 16,200 feet. Stephen also said that they do miss home and, yet each of them is filled with gratitude that they are here and immersed in such an amazing experience. They will send another update in a couple of days.

The post didn't accurately describe Jeff's condition or the doctor's concerns about my blood pressure, but there was no denying the energy of the climb or the gratitude we felt at getting even as far as we had. And, yes, seeing Aconcagua in the distance was enough to take any man's breath away. Its snow-capped and jagged peaks formed the spine of a seriously intimidating mountain range.

At this point, I began to fall in love with the beauty of this mountain. I really loved her. She was gorgeous. I also knew, however, that she could crush any of us with her rage at any moment. While it may sound odd, I began to talk to her. I honored her beauty and respected her strength. She was a combination of both grace and power. A sense of awe and excitement was sprinkled with anticipation and trepidation. Were we really going to climb her? Hell, yes we were!

The night of the sixth day was spent packing everything each man intended to carry to the next camp,

High Camp 1, which was at an altitude of 16,300 feet above sea-level and a full half-mile higher than any of us had climbed.

———

**Our instructions were simple.
Prepare as if your life depends on it.**

———

We had to think ahead and ask ourselves what gear we wouldn't need the following night—which would be spent back in Base Camp—or during the "move" the following day.

We also had to keep in mind that the mules that had carried so much of our gear during the three-day-trek to Base Camp could go no higher, so that luxury was no longer at our disposal. We knew we had to factor food and water into the equation, along with all of our gear.

The Aconcagua Man Project equipment list, which you will find in the Appendix at the end of this book, was shockingly complete. I was amazed when I first saw what each of us would be hauling. I took it on faith that it would all be necessary, and gazing on the rugged, merciless mountain awaiting our arrival, I was glad I had.

The list suggests rather strongly why our packs weighed anywhere from fifty to sixty pounds.

———

**It did not pay to get caught on a mountain like
Aconcagua without the essentials, and most of what we
were carrying had been deemed essential.**

———

The clouds and the wind arrived late in the afternoon of our rest day, but by then, we were expecting it. There was a hint of snow in the air as we packed our gear, but there was no accumulation to speak of.

I didn't sleep particularly well that night. I wanted to remember the dreams that invaded what little sleep I got, but it was not to be.

Breaking New Ground

After a breakfast of scrambled eggs, toast, and Yerba mate, we set out. The route started off as a slippery scree slope. The footing was difficult almost from the beginning, and we got our first taste of the mountain's nasty side. Even as the route went up a gentle trail on the rocky, moraine-covered Relinchos Glacier, I could see everyone concentrating on their steps, nine men in a line, a cohesive unit suddenly immersed in the task at hand. Each step was like walking on the moon. It was surreal and beautiful, like a moving meditation.

The path along the face of the rock field is narrow, and straying from it is not a good idea. The glacier is situated between Cerro Aconcagua and Cerro Ameghino, which are the Argentinians' names for Aconcagua and the neighboring Ameghino. Cerro, I discover, means "hill." It's hard not to find this ironic, but maybe they're referring mostly to Ameghino, which is only 17,651 feet high. The vista is breathtaking in a rugged, moonscape sort of way; all grays, silvers, muted browns, and carved surfaces sprinkled with broken rock.

The spirits of the team are good for the most part, even though there is minimal conversation.

No one is quieter than Jeff, and I'm worried about him. He's taken up a position near the rear of the line along with Gusto, and this is to become a   habit going forward.

Eric, Troy, and Vince all move with a steady, easy pace with Rolo in the lead, and I can see that this stretch of the climb is coming easily to them. Vince likes to call out the changing altitude as he tracks it on his GPS, and I can imagine this getting annoying further along the line.

Greg is struggling. Even with his poles, he's having trouble with his gait. This is something we had worked on during all of our training hikes: evenly distributing our weight, taking short steps, and minimizing the strain on our calf muscles. It's hard to do so with fifty pounds on our backs, but it's essential to keep the wear and tear on our bodies to a minimum. Greg was my college roommate. He and I have over thirty years of history, off and on. In all those years, I had never known him to be so quiet. I could tell the silent killer had his mind and body in a grip. Still, he was focused and pushed upward.

Dennis has his climbing technique down perfectly, and I'm in awe of his strength and agility at sixty-seven years old. In my mind's eye, I can see Dennis on the summit, and the image is inspiring.

As for me, I have a video camera in my hand, and the task is helping me keep my mind off the blood pressure issue I'm dealing with. My feet hurt, but it's tolerable. I

142

tell myself to keep moving, to focus on each step, and to allow myself to take in the beauty of this moment. That was the easy part.

We come upon an extraordinary anomaly called Nieve Penitentes: a formation of snow and ice that looks, from a distance, like an army of white robed figures marching along the valley floor. Closer to it, the river of silver and white brings to mind a huge honeycomb or a field of stalactites punching through the earth's skin. The snow accumulations, Mike tells us, can rise as high as twenty feet, though they're closer to the height of a man on this day. They are remarkable and eerie. I sweep my camera over them, and we pause long enough for an energy bar and a water break.

We press on, a switchback taking us into another rock scree field. The wind kicks up, and snow blows like angel dust from the rocks.

――――

At this point, we're doing serious climbing.

――――

Your concentration level as you move up and across the rocks has to be at a high level, because a simple misstep could send you tumbling. The possibilities of a sprained ankle or worse are very real.

As we approach 16,000 feet, the jagged peaks on either side of the valley gather a veil of clouds that remind us how quickly the weather can change at this high atmosphere. When we reach High Camp I, we bivouac the majority of our gear in preparation for our return the following day. We pause long enough for a meal—

sandwiches and cookies—and water, a commodity that becomes increasingly precious the higher we climb.

Before we set out, I spent a long minute peering up at the massive west face of Aconcagua, still a brutal, exhausting, 7,000-foot rise away, and all I could feel was exhilaration.

I realized, staring up at Cerro Aconcagua, that the task at hand was formidable, but the exhilaration made the task worthwhile. This mountain was clarifying that the work I was doing back home and the relationships I was pursuing were the product of the same type of exhilaration.

Many of us have resigned ourselves to the debilitating belief that we cannot have a life filled with a certain amount of excitement and joy. I think that is crazy. Without that, you're priming a dry well. Without that, your work can't really be inspired. Finding your personal "Aconcagua" can bring excitement to your life and to your relationships. You owe it to yourself to find it. With respect to my work back home, I realized that the cooperative leadership model that I was developing with clients every day could only be driven to the next level if I was steering those clients toward enterprises that challenged and inspired them. They would be better leaders, and they would also be more successful as businessmen and human beings. That was the whole point.

Every "Aconcagua" endeavor, big or small, adventurous or practical, has to be integrated into our lives afterward in the most positive way possible, and this integration influences our personal lives and our professional lives as well as our world view.

You can't come away from an "Aconcagua" experience without sharing it out in the world.

Otherwise, the growth and change that you went into the endeavor expecting to generate will never come to fruition.

That's part of breaking new ground.

Expect the Unexpected.

With a far lighter load on our backs, we head back down the mountain. We make Base Camp in two hours. It's nearly dinnertime. We gather in our mess tent. The carry day puts the realities of the mountain into perspective. It's an amazing day, and I have a feeling that none of us will ever be the same from this day forward. None of us, save Eric Wiseman, had ever before been above 14,000 feet. We have broken new ground.

I study our team, watching their faces and listening to their voices.

Dennis and Eric are both projecting optimism. Vince is calm and focused. Troy shares openly with the group this night. I enjoy hearing more about his past. Jeff can't shake his headache, and he looks a bit drawn. Greg's levity is a welcome gift. Our guides give us the low down about the "move" day tomorrow, and I 'm excited to press on.

I sleep better, knowing I've already experienced the higher altitude at Camp I and come away from it no worse for wear. We don't get under way the next morning until after nine o'clock, but the weather holds, for the most part, during our hike back up to Camp I, and we arrive with

145

most of the afternoon left to set up our tents and get prepared for a night at 16,300 feet. The wind is already starting to blow as we prepare a dinner of polenta and noodles. There is always Mate and there is always tea, and both are welcome.

––––––

**We are all donning our cold weather gear now,
and most of us are inside our tents by eight-thirty,
simply because it's too cold to be outside.**

––––––

I am thankful for my Thermarest pad and my sleeping bag once we've settled in. The bag is good to twenty degrees below zero.
I write in my journal while Jeff reads. We talk some, mostly about how we're both feeling. I'm okay. He's not so good.
I don't know what time it is when I finally fall asleep. I dream that Greg has decided to quit the climb, and I wake up with a start around two o'clock in the morning. The wind is shaking the tent. I sip water, turn over in my bag, and manage a couple more hours of sleep. I have to take a pee and don't want to go outside. I use my designated pee bottle and try not to wake Jeff. We're standing around eating breakfast when Greg calls us all together.

13 GREG'S ACONCAGUA

It's January 27, our tenth day in Argentina.

One by one, the team responds to Greg's call for a team meeting, each of them with a hot drink in their hand. It's chilly, but I forget about the cold as I watch Greg's face. I have the feeling that he is about to drop a bomb on us.

I'm right.

"I have something I need to tell you guys," he begins. He looks tired, but no worse for wear than any of the rest of us. "I'm going back down the mountain. This is my summit."

Everyone is equally shocked, and why not? We've really just begun; the real climb is still ahead of us. Other than Greg's discomfort on the mountain yesterday, there has been no indication that he is in distress. I hear someone say, "What's up?" and it may well have been me.

"I'm not breathing well. I haven't been able to sleep. It just doesn't feel right," he said. "This is it for me. I don't mean to break up the team, but this is a decision I've made."

I listen as Greg's teammates have their say, one by one, as if it is mandatory for each of us to share our feelings with Greg. I hear disappointment in the men's voices. I hear disbelief, and I can completely empathize. I hear logic and have a litany of logical reasons why Greg should reconsider his decision. I find myself listening to every word people are saying, but Greg really isn't. His mind is made up.

He says, "I've made my decision. I appreciate everything you guys are saying, but I'm not changing my mind. If I've learned one thing in working with Stephen over the last year, it's to be clear in my decisions. And I'm clear about this."

"Greg, why don't you come up with me as far as High Camp," Dennis says. "And then you and I will come down together from there."

Here is Dennis once again suggesting that High Camp would be an acceptable end to his climb—something I hear loud and clear, though I'm not sure the rest of the group does—but Greg isn't open to the idea. "I appreciate it, Dennis. It would be fun descending with you. But no."

"This is my summit, Eric. I want to get back to my family."

"Listen, Greg, you're the guy who's always been there for all of us," Jeff said. "You're the guy who's always giving us a lift when we need it the most. You've been dragging me up the mountain since we first began. Why don't you let us do that for you for a while? Give it a day or two to get your strength back. It's okay to feel a little vulnerable, man. That's something we have all learned."

Greg isn't really listening. In fact, I can see that he's not going to budge. "No thanks. I've already decided."

148

Our guide, Mike Bradley, steps in right there and throws out a completely logical suggestion. He says, "How about this, Greg? Why don't you help us carry to Camp II? It's about 1,200 further up. See how you feel. Give yourself the day to think about it. When we come back down this afternoon, make a decision then."

I'm glad Mike has spoken up, because nothing the team has said is having any effect. Greg agrees, probably because it's Mike who is making the suggestion. I'm disappointed, mostly because I know Greg could make the summit. I also know that his family is the most important thing in his life right now. I think the team wants to understand something more than Greg has shared, and yet I respect his decision and tell him that. Each man is ultimately responsible for his own life, and, at the end of the day, we all must respect that.

"As long as you're clear," I say.

"I'm clear," he replies.

We prepare for our carry day to Camp II at an altitude of 17,500. Greg carries his share, and I can see in his step that one more day isn't going to change his mind. We're losing one of our teammates. We will all miss him on the journey upward.

We climb 700 feet to an altitude of 17,000 feet and stop for lunch. We're just finishing up when Greg takes his place up in front of the group once again and announces his decision to return to Camp I right there and then. He'll get his stuff together and wait for us there.

"It doesn't make any sense to me to go any higher. I hope you guys understand."

Greg would later lament not staying with us throughout the carry day to Camp II, but I don't think anyone held it against him. After all, we had to concentrate on several more hours of hard climbing.

"See you when we come back to High Camp I," I said. We shook hands. "Don't get lost."

We set out one man short. Greg watches us go. Our route settles upon the back of a flat, eroded slab of rock called the Ameghino saddle. A gentle traverse takes us to the Guanacos Valley and an extraordinary view of the Polish Glacier, a mammoth slab of ice and slow that rises 3,000 feet up the side of the mountain. The Polish Route takes climbers within spitting distance of the glacier, but it's a more difficult and risky route and less prone to success. Our plan is to use what is called the Upper Guanacos Traverse, a slightly less technical route, even if just as taxing.

Smart Risk

There is no shortage of risk when you make the decision to climb a mountain that soars 22,834 in the air. Many people have died climbing Aconcagua. It's dangerous. You cannot predict the weather at that altitude. There is no easy way out once you're this high. There are sheer cliff faces. There are rock fields that invite accidents, even for the most focused hiker. There is altitude sickness. There is pulmonary and cerebral edema.

Every "Aconcagua" endeavor comes with risks. Whatever your Aconcagua is, count on it having associated risks. You don't change careers or start a new business without risk. You don't build positive relationships without risk. You don't make a statement in the world with your actions without risk.

We knew the odds when we decided to make a run at the summit of the highest peak in the world outside of

150

Asia. Two-thirds of all the people who set out from Mendoza return without the bragging rights that come from stepping on the summit. Those aren't great odds. Preparation, planning, and hard work improve the odds. Attitude and conviction also improve the odds.

The question is, do you take the risk, or do you give into expecting the bad outcome before you even start? I can tell you that most people choose the latter. But I can also tell you that the people who take the risk and follow their dreams are stronger and more inspired for having done so.

Men used to be known as the risk-takers of our society. Now many men have allowed themselves to be shackled by the voice of society telling them to be safe and secure, even if it means being unfulfilled.

I hoped that Greg wouldn't feel that way when he got back to Denver. I hoped that he was authentic in calling 17,000 feet his Aconcagua summit. Before our trip, Greg had written:

> *As I really look into what the Aconcagua Man Project is all about and why I personally joined it, the following questions jump out. Where are my limits? What can I achieve personally, physically, spiritually, and emotionally if I truly apply all my learning AND train myself to listen to a higher calling? What/where is my true potential relative to service and inspiration to other?*

I hoped he would come away from the experience with answers to these questions. While I personally wanted Greg to continue on up the mountain, I respected him for his dogged clarity. None of us can ever really know what lies in another man's heart. I think for Greg, he just wanted to be with his family.

The Beat Goes On

We ascend a nasty scree slope to the crest of a broad ridge. The snow here is fresh and deep, and the air is so crisp that it stings at first. We establish High Camp II in a sheltered nook. The six of us move with purpose and ease, mooring our carry gear before the descent back to Camp I.

Greg is there to meet us. He's in good spirits. We take a couple of team photos, in exactly the same order as we have done throughout: me, Greg, Troy, Eric, Jeff, Dennis, and Vince. We take pictures of Greg with the blue and yellow stuffed bears that he'd promised his kids he would carry to the summit. He charges Troy and me with the task of getting the bears to the top, and I have to say I feel honored to have been asked. I know Troy does; I think that he'll miss Greg more than anyone.

Greg settles into the routine of the evening meal, and he seems relaxed again, as if making the decision has freed his spirit. He has some private words with several of the team members, but the exchanges are more about missing his presence than about trying to change his mind.

In the morning, we pack up our tents for the move to Camp II. We say our goodbyes. I leave Greg with a bear hug. Our Aconcagua team is now six in number. Because Aventuras Patagonicas requires everyone on the mountain to be in the company of one of their mountaineering guides, Gusto agrees to accompany Greg back down to Mendoza. So now, our guide team consists only of Rolo and Mike.

Move day got underway just before ten o'clock in the morning, on the 28th, under a resoundingly blue sky and a white-hot sun. The upper Guanacos Valley runs like a chute between walls of jagged stone. The path is wide enough for one man, and we stretched out in single-file: Rolo in the lead, with Troy, and Eric and me close behind. Jeff, Dennis, and Vince brought up the rear.

Vince has evolved. When we first hit the mountain, nine days ago, he was still trying to find his place among the guys. He may even have been trying a little too hard. But right from the beginning, he put the team first. Every day, as the climbs grew more difficult, I saw him become more and more of an asset. When anyone needed help with his gear, he was there. When it looked like someone was experiencing difficulties on the climb, he made himself available.

There was a time when Vince preferred soloing on a mountain. The day before he had told me how much he was enjoying the team experience, and it showed. Vince was in the throes of a divorce when he signed on for the climb, and he would tell me later how cathartic the climb was for him. It opened a door on the guilt and the anger he had been holding onto, and he had finally allowed himself to grieve.

I, for one, am extremely glad he had chosen to join us on the climb, even if it was late in the game, and I think the rest of the guys are feeling very much the same way by this time.

———

It is interesting how much of leadership these days is about bringing together a group of diverse personalities and molding a team that works well together and produces results.

———

153

It's no different on Aconcagua than it is in the workplace. A manager can't force an atmosphere of collaboration onto the members of his or her team. The manager has to create an environment where every individual sees value in working well with the others. He has to ferret out the individual strengths of the members of the team and help them channel those strengths. But even as he's doing that, he has to expect them all to perform at a high level. When they do, he lets them know.

We walk until just past noon and take a short break to refuel and hydrate. The sun is high in the sky, and we're able to get away with our hooded, windproof, outer jackets. Hats, sunglasses, and sunscreen are absolutely essential. We don't need the crampons on our double mountaineering boots yet, but everyone relies on ski poles, except for Rolo.

We make Camp II by mid-afternoon. The first task, as always, is to get our tents set up. The next task is to get water: melt it, drink it, and store it.

Dinner is pasta, and everyone of us is starving. We have a team meeting. Mike talks about the next step in our journey; a climb of nearly 1,800 feet to High Camp III at an altitude of 19,200 feet. Our already steep climb is about to get even steeper and more precarious. The plan is to traverse from the saddle to the upper Guanacos and then up the east face. I listen . My mouth is dry and my heart rate jumps a couple of beats. I can see on the faces of my teammates that they're feeling very much the same. We realize that 19,000 feet is 5,000 feet higher than any of us had ever climbed.

Mike cautions us. It will be cold: ten degrees at most, and below zero when the wind blows.

"And plan on the wind blowing," he says. "We'll be climbing. Plan on a tough day." The weather, he tells us, will be a huge factor, and could even determine how far we go and whether or not we keep going. Mike has been driven off the mountain by the weather before. He's not trying to scare us; he wants us to be prepared.

A storm moves in that evening, and the wind picks up. We know it's going to happen, but a temperature drop is always startling. We pair up and move in the direction of our tents: Troy and Jeff, Vince and Eric, and Dennis and me.

14 FORTIFIED COMMITMENT

Sleep does not come easily when you're at altitude. You're told this. You research it. You come to expect it.

You hear reports of excessively vivid dreams, and I was having them every night. You hear stories of climbers who swear they're suffocating, and both Troy and Jeff had episodes of this. High altitude can also produce something called "periodic breathing," which involves alternating periods of deep breathing and shallow breathing, and Greg sounded as if he may have been a victim of that.

————

My body found a zone. I'd had almost no sleep, but the adrenaline of the day had made my body feel alive and vital.

————

Part of these symptoms could be attributed to altitude sickness, which was not surprising given the low oxygen levels we were experiencing. Part of these symptoms could also be attributed to the cold and the wind, and we were experiencing our fair share of both, especially at night.

And if your tent mate snored or was constantly moving during the night, you could put part of the blame on him.

It didn't matter what the reason was if you woke up at the crack of dawn and felt as if you hadn't slept a wink. We all had nights that were like that during the climb. But it wasn't as if you could turn over and go back to sleep.

Rest days are different, but this is not a rest day. We're on the move, and the day calls. We dress in our tents, remembering that today is a carry day to High Camp. The key to this "carry" is anticipating what would be needed when we return to Camp II for the night. I put on lightweight, synthetic, long underwear and breathable windproof pants. I put on silk inner socks and wool outside socks. I put on double mountaineering boots and knee-high gaiters.

I also put on an expedition-weight thermal, a fleece jacket, and a Gore-Tex outer-jacket. I know I'll want my Polarguard expedition parka with the insulated hood when the sun goes down later, but it will probably be too much for the hike during the day. The parka is good to 20 degrees below zero. Because the temperature will drop well below zero at this altitude, most of us have taken to wearing our parkas to bed. I'll want it here when we return, so my plan is to leave it in my tent.

Prioritization
Setting priorities is one of the most conscious things we do on the mountain, and our priorities change the higher the climb takes us.

Suddenly, the rock basketball games that had occupied our rest stops earlier on are the furthest thing from our minds, simply because they take too much energy. Suddenly, the running conversations that had filled

158

the hours before we got to Base Camp have abdicated to minimal exchanges focused on things like making sure we have enough water or reminders about our gear. We think about every step at 17,500 feet. We think about chewing every bite of our food a little more thoroughly. Sleep, warmth, and nourishment climb higher on our priority list, along with the continual monitoring of our mental and physical health.

What the rarified air at altitude does is change our priorities to be those things that can most influence our success. What do we have to do? And what is less important?

Life is like that as well. Whether it's work or play, our priorities are based upon the clarity of the values that we adhere to as men; the values that we commit to as human beings.

The more you consciously prioritize, the more likely you are to find success in your endeavors. If your goal is having a six-handicap on the golf course, time on the practice range should probably take priority over watching golf on television. If your goal is running a twenty million dollar company three years after launch, getting your product from the drawing board to the production floor should probably take priority over remodeling your rec room.

———

When things are meaningful to you, knowing how to prioritize them comes naturally.

———

The litmus test of whether you're really committed to an endeavor is how you align your priorities in the long run. What's important to you? Think of what hinges upon that question. Very likely, it's the success or failure of your own personal "Aconcagua," much like it was for us. Know what's important to you, and then act upon it.

It's cold when Dennis and I climb out of our tent. Rolo has already started breakfast: oatmeal and dried fruit, hot tea or coffee, and an energy bar and water. Always water.

———

Everyone is responsible for loading up his own pack for a carry day, though everyone will help out if someone needs a hand.

———

Eric and Troy routinely carry sixty pounds on their backs. Vince and I shoulder packs that were nearly as heavy, and I think back on all the hikes we had taken in Colorado with full packs. The training is paying off. On the mountain, your team is responsible for everything from garbage and trash to the state-issued plastic bags designated for bathroom waste.

Jeff is hurting. It takes him a very long time to do anything. We do what we can to help, but mostly we're patient. I am amazed at his persistence. We've spent days on the mountain, and Jeff has been fighting his body the entire time: headaches, nausea, and dizziness. But he has never complained. From day one, he has shown the qualities of a collaborative leader, engaging his teammates with conversation, laughter, and encouragement. Jeff is a life coach, in fact, he's the "go to" coach in Aspen Colorado, so he is adept at practicing the mental focus he teaches to his own clients. He listens deeply and shares

160

openly. He doesn't give advice unless advice is asked for. These skills haven't diminished here on the mountain, despite his discomfort.

Jeff had told me back at Camp I that he'd stopped resisting the headaches and the nausea. "I'm realizing that it's part of the process, and I decided I wasn't going to get anything out of the process if I didn't start accepting it."

Jeff was right about that, and I was impressed enough with his attitude that I made it part of my own mindset. Resisting the process only makes things harder. It doesn't matter what you're striving to accomplish. When you resist, you're not open. The less open you are, the less you'll take away from the experience. Sometimes it's painful. Sometimes the pain is physical, but just as often it is emotional or spiritual. When there is suffering involved, self-honesty about the reasons and the causes is the only antidote. It's the only way to grow.

We leave our tents and our essential night gear behind and hit the trail at just after eight o'clock in the morning.

It is a spectacular day. The temperature is ten degrees in the sun. Any gust of wind drives that number down to zero or below, in the blink of an eye.

No one really complains about the temperature, however, because we have the necessary gear to keep us warm. I remember some of us looked with a bit of a cynical eye at the fifty or so items on Eric Wiseman's equipment list last fall, but no one is anything but grateful the higher into the Andes we travel . In that regard, Eric has accomplished one of his goals in spades. He has prepared us at a world-class level. And more than that, I am continually grateful for his pleasant and steady demeanor on the mountain.

We trudge through six inches of snow, but my feet are never cold. We are wearing insulated and windproof gloves with GORE-TEX© shells, and my hands are as warm as toast all day.

———

Halfway through the morning, the upper Guanacos opens up onto an awe-inspiring vista of Aconcagua and it takes our breath away.

———

Jagged, harsh, and magnificent, the peak spirals upward into a bank of clouds. The Polish Glacier forms a skirt of blinding white up one side.

Looking at it from afar, the very idea of climbing to the top seems like an impossible task. Its face is solid rock, glazed with ice and snow.

We know there's a well-defined path winding to the summit, but we'd need high-powered binoculars to see it from here. We all stop and stare. This is why we'd come, and the pit opening up in my stomach makes me appreciate the moment even more.

Mike describes the ascent like a professor dissecting a routine physics problem. He points, and we try to follow his directions.

"From High Camp to the summit is a 2,000-foot climb. One day, up and down," he says. The planned summit day is January 31, but our schedule allows for an extra day if we run into problems. "But that's a couple of days away. Let's take it one step at a time and hope the weather holds."

A part of me wants to forget about a carry day. I want to get to High Camp right away and prepare for the 2,000-

foot climb Mike was describing to us. I think, let's get to it. But another part of me—a stronger, more focused part —tells me to relax, enjoy the journey, and enjoy the process.

Here's the thing. Every "Aconcagua" endeavor is a journey: a process. There aren't very many things in life worth accomplishing where you can set the goal and accomplish it without hard work and the sweat equity, the highs and the lows, the growth, and the change. If you can, then it probably doesn't qualify as an "Aconcagua" endeavor. With that in mind, I'll ask you again: What is your Aconcagua? And what are you willing to do to make it happen?

———

Whether it's personal or professional, you face the obstacles as they come along because you see the prize at the end.

———

Sometimes the obstacles can be overcome. Sometimes they can't. An "Aconcagua" endeavor isn't defined by success or failure. There is always gain. There is always growth. Integration is inevitable.

Fear and Pain
There is something vastly inspiring about being high above the rest of the world, somewhere that seems a lifetime away from civilization and security and predictability. There is also something extraordinarily intimidating. There is nothing in our line of sight as we pass 18,000 feet, except a world of high peaks captured in scrims of cloud and mist.

Fear can be utilized to fortify commitment. Great moments are often defined by how an individual uses his or her fear.

———

We know that people die on this mountain. We know that people suffer debilitating injuries. We know that every man, no matter how strong he is, is susceptible to physical stresses that even nine months of intense training cannot always prepare him for. But we don't let those sorts of thoughts drift too closely to the surface, because that is a step away from paralysis.

Instead, we keep moving.

A body changes when it's breathing very thin air. Every step takes effort. Every step taxes strength and endurance, and fifty or sixty pounds on the back doesn't help matters. We don't hurry because we can't. The body won't let that happen. We are on a single track traversing rock and snow, so our focus is on the trail and the man in front of us.

We don't talk, because there's not really enough air, and we really don't have the strength or the inclination. Someone says, "This is extraordinary up here, isn't it?" Someone says, "How you doing?" Someone says, "Are we having fun yet?" That's about it.

I find myself experiencing waves of emotional and spiritual shifts, and I embrace them with open arms.

Gratitude is one of the feelings. I have thought about this endeavor for years, and now I'm here with as fine a group of men as I could have imagined and all the planning and persistence is paying off. I find myself feeling enlivened and powerful, as if there is really nothing I can't achieve if I really put my mind to it. I feel this rather intimate connection with my higher power, and I allow myself to slip into an inner dialogue with him. It's genuinely moving.

The higher we climb, the more I have to focus on each step, and the more I realize that each man is more or less on his own up this high. You can't walk in someone else's shoes even if you help shoulder some of their burden. Being part of a team at this stage is more about holding up your own end. You know that if everyone does his own part, the whole has a better chance of succeeding.

In life, sometimes holding up your own end is all you can ask of yourself. Maybe that's one definition of responsibility, but most men are more self-fulfilled when they can lend a hand to others.

Service is a way of being a man.
It becomes engrained into the heart and soul.
Once integrated, it will fortify us to no end.

At this stage in the climb, I have a need to get creative. Climbing for hours on end, or lying in your tent, there is a lot of time for thinking. Some of those thoughts are powerful and others, well, are not so much. I decide to create a meditation of sorts as I climb. I think of all the people in my life that I love: my family, my friends, my clients, my teammates, my spiritual teachers, and even my past relationships. Each step I take, I speak a name in my mind. My right foot might be "Doug," for my brother. Then my left foot will be "McGhee." It is so powerful. All

165

at once, I'm climbing for people I care about. I'm surprised at how much this helps; it's as if I were taking these people up the mountain with me.

Our team is stretched out across the mountain at this point. Jeff has fallen further back, and Rolo climbs with him. I turn on my camera and run several minutes of footage, allowing Eric and Troy to move past me, their steps as slow and persistent as turtles scaling a sandy beach, one step in front of another.

Eric smiles. There is something special going on with him. I can almost see the personal discoveries building up, one after another, on his face and in his eyes. I almost see a new man emerging, and I have to rejoice for him. I'm already looking forward to some one-on-one time when the climb is over.

Troy is like a single-minded machine with a singular purpose. He glances at the camera, and I see someone who won't allow himself to stop or lose focus. Aconcagua is a proving ground for Troy, and I have a feeling his integration, once we return, will be chaotic and challenging.

I can see on Vince's face as he moves past me that this is not his best day. I want to reach out to him. I manage a pat on the back and hope it communicates the empathy I'm feeling.

Dennis is not far behind, and there is something in his posture that reflects the willpower of a man who has taken on hundreds of challenges in his life and managed a degree of success in each and every one of them. I also see a sixty-seven-year-old man who had often talked to me during our training days about knowing our limits.

**Dennis says, "What a day, huh, Stephen?"
And he's right:
It's a day none of us will ever forget.**

Just then, the wind funnels down the mountain: a wicked blast that reminds me that we still have to stow our gear at High Camp and return once again to Camp II. Jeff and Rolo are a hundred yards further back, and I turn the camera on them for ten seconds. Rolo gives me a brief wave.

I move the camera across a broad sweep of gray, white, and brilliant blue: stone, snow, and sky. Then I give my attention back to the trail and begin my meditation again, while putting one foot in front of the other. "A step for God. A step for me."

We reach High Camp at 19,200 feet above sea level early in the afternoon. The site is called Piedras Blancas (the White Rocks), and compared to the grays, blacks, and silvers of the surrounding stone, the name fits. The stunning view threatens to take my breath away. The snow-capped peaks of the Andes reach all the way to the horizon.

We take only as much time as we need to eat a power bar, drink from the water we had melted that morning, and stow our gear at the designated campsite.

High Camp is one step from the top of the world, but that one step is still a brutally steep climb of 3,000 feet. This is rarified air for even the most experienced mountaineer. There is a feeling of awe and excitement, oddly melded with a trace of disorientation. It's almost as if we can feel the earth moving under our feet.

I check the team's pulse as we prepare to descend back to Camp II and another night of acclimatization.

I sense some discomfort brewing up in Dennis, and I wonder if he's feeling all right. Or could he be anxious? Dennis had invited Greg Aden to climb as far as High Camp with him, and then the two of them would descend together. I hoped it wouldn't turn into a self-fulfilling prophecy—less Greg, of course—but I also know how hard it is to separate yourself from your intentions.

Jeff is just glad to have a moment to sit down, but there is also an expectant glimmer in his eye. I think he's shocked to have made it this high, but I'm not surprised at all. Jeff has that internal fire that so many men lack. I've seen it back in the real world, and I've seen it here on the mountain.

Eric is like a kid in a candy store. His excitement is clearly balanced by a sense of unexpected discovery. It's as if the impulses are coming fast and furious, and he's trying to make sense of them.

Troy is tough to read. He's created his own private world for himself on the climb. I think it's given him strength, but he's difficult to penetrate when he chooses to go within. I don't think failing to summit is an option for Troy.

Vince is hurting. He's fighting himself emotionally and physically. By the time we make it back to Camp II, he's shedding tears. But I can tell that they are good tears, cathartic tears. We all give him his space. I now know what is welling up within him. He is grieving his recent divorce. I feel for him. We all do. The team has created a space for the miraculous, and Vince is experiencing a miracle right now. There is some good conversation during dinner. Nothing deep or philosophical, but grounding. I talk about my excitement for what's ahead, but I also share the pride I feel for our team. I wouldn't want to be there with anyone else, not after all we'd gone through together.

We turn in early, but the night is restless. I try to write. I try reading a book. I wouldn't mind talking to Jeff, but he's already fallen into a deep sleep. Instead, I let my mind wander. I hear a voice in my head saying, "You're different from when you left. You're evolving."

I don't analyze it. I don't need to. I know it's a good thing. I have fortified my commitment to all things important to me.

15 REACHING THE SUMMIT AND BEYOND

If everything goes according to schedule, we will summit on February 1, twelve days after we'd set out from Penitentes. What primarily affects the schedule is the weather, which can turn ugly in the blink of an eye. The health of the team also plays a hand in it, and it's best to expect the unexpected.

Move day went smoothly. It was bitterly cold, but the sun was bright white and the sky was beyond blue. We ascended the North West Ridge back to High Camp. We threw our tents up, taking special pains in staking them down.

There are two or three other groups making their preparations for a summit bid tomorrow, so we will have a certain amount of company. This isn't unusual for this time of the year. December, January, and February present the most opportune windows for conquering the great mountain, though "conquer" is hardly an appropriate term.

**You "thrive" to the summit, if you're lucky.
Most aren't.**

There is a palpable excitement in the air as we melt snow and fire up the camp stoves for a meal of soup and noodles. There is also a tendril of anxiety, caused by staring at the upper slopes of Aconcagua, which appear impervious and uninviting in the last light of day.

We make final preparations for our summit day: food, water, and gear. We carry only what we need for a full twelve hours on the move, but always, always with an unbridled appreciation for how swiftly and brutally the weather can change.

This is how I think about it. Upper body: expedition weight synthetic shirt, heavy fleece jacket, heavyweight polar guard expedition parka with insulated hood, good to 20 below. Lower body: expedition weight Capilene© long underwear, fleece pants, breathable windproof bibs with full-length side zippers. Hands: insulated, windproof, fingered gloves and insulated over-mitts specifically selected for summit day. Head: wool ski hat, sunglasses, and ski goggles. Feet: inner and outer socks, plastic double mountaineering boots, and 12-point, non-rigid crampons.

We go to bed that night to the news that Mike has a bad feeling about the weather. The winds are stirring, and the clouds are trundling, over the high peaks of the Andes from the north.

172

The forecast isn't favorable.

Mike confers with Rolo and confers with the team, but the decision rests entirely with him. There are contingencies built into our schedule: an extra summit day in case a storm closes down the mountain.

"We're resting tomorrow," he tells us.

We secure everything, double-checking our tent stakes, and preparing for the worst. I'm okay with the decision, because I am respectful of Mike's experience.

All hell breaks loose. We retreat to our tents: Jeff and me in one, Vince and Dennis in another, and Eric and Troy in theirs. By early morning the next day, I'm giving thanks for Mike's decision. The wind is literally howling. Snow falls in horizontal streaks across the mountain.

In a bomber-squared tent the size of a walk-in closet with 75 mph winds and 100 mph gusts pounding the mountain, you begin to wonder how long the urethane-coated mesh can hold up. It's unnerving; you know hundreds of people every year are literally driven back down the mountain by winds just like these.

We are literally pinned down for 18 hours.

We don't give up hope of a summit day the next day, but we realize it would not be an option if the weather doesn't break. We forget about sleep. We forget about reading or writing. The constant roar makes conversation

173

difficult even with a man who is lying in a sleeping bag a foot away. On the other hand, there is not much to say. I try my best to rest...

I've talked a lot about leadership during this nine-month odyssey: in many ways, the primary focus of the entire Aconcagua Man Project has been about how to lead in the most productive way possible. I tried to create an atmosphere for the team where leading and learning came together as inseparable parts of the same process. Collaborative leadership is, first and foremost, about creating an atmosphere that says, "We're all in this together."

Or are we? Late in afternoon of the rest day, with the winds howling, Vince sticks his head in my tent. I can see the look of concern on his face even before he speaks. "Dennis is in bad shape. There's no way he can summit tomorrow," he tells us.

Mike joins Vince and me in their tent. Dennis doesn't look good. He is so weak, and his head is pounding so badly, that he can hardly sip water. He is worried about cerebral edema and has already made up his mind that he won't go up in the morning. I am a little bit shocked, because Dennis seemed so strong up to High Camp. He is tenacity personified. He is a remarkable meld of wisdom and youthful enthusiasm. And here he is calling High Camp his summit.

"I'll go down with a porter," he says. "That way the team will still have two guides going forward. I want you all to summit."

Dennis has thought this out. He doesn't want to sacrifice our chances of making the summit by leaving us with a single guide. That is Dennis through and through. As surprised as I might be, I am also okay with his

174

decision. I think it is the right one, and I tell him so. "As long as you promise me one thing," I say, as he begins to close his blood-stained eyes.

"What's that?"

"That you won't judge yourself down the road for not going to the top. That you can truly be satisfied with calling this your summit."

Dennis promises me that, and I want to believe him. I also know just how competitive he is, which means it might be a hard promise for him to keep. I also know that Dennis, Greg, and the whole team will be with us, even if just in spirit, if and when we do summit.

**The Aconcagua Man Project, after all,
is not an ego quest.**

The quest isn't about a summit 22,834 feet above sea level. It is far more about learning. It is about the acute understanding of what it means to reach your personal summit. It is also about understanding that any decision rendered in recognition of your personal summit represents one of the most powerful decisions a man can ever make.

When you realize that, suddenly everyone on your team—whether it's on a mountain at 19,200 feet or in the offices of your very large company—every member of your team has a sense of ownership in whatever goal you've set: a place where team alignment becomes more important than team agreement. In the case of Dennis and Greg, I was not happy, because I selfishly wanted our whole team to get to the top. On the other hand, I understood both their decisions.

175

**A man's job is to shed light in this world.
A man's job is to create experiences and to
infuse as much energy as he can into them.**

———

I try to keep that in mind as the night tarries on, fraying my nerves and punching holes in our resolve.

At four o'clock in the morning, almost to the second, Mother Nature flips a switch, and the winds suddenly, miraculously dies down. I am lying in the tent next to Jeff. In the blink of an eye, it is over. The silence is, as the saying goes, truly deafening.

Twenty-four minutes later—I know this to the minute because I am looking at my watch—I hear the cook stoves in the guides' tent fire up. I know what this means. We are summit-bound. Our first task is to get dressed and our second task is to try and eat something. Mike and Rolo are melting snow for water. Rolo gives each of us a frozen pound cake and two liters of water for the day.

Clarified Air

They refer to the air at this altitude as "rarified," simply because there is so little oxygen in it and because it is so clean and so pure.

As we ready our packs for our run at the Aconcagua's summit and check-list our gear, I gaze out at one of the most dynamic, compelling sunrises a man could ever see. The vapor and mist rise off the snow and ice and paint the morning like a mythical dream world.

―――――

**The words come to me in what really
is a rush of emotion: clarified air.**

―――――

This isn't a play on words, but rather a way of thinking. To see where you've been and where you're going without all the encumbrances of society's poisonous expectations, to claim ownership of your purpose without needing the approval of anyone else, to recognize that success is being at peace with who and what you are, to make no apology about it, and to be willing to share your gifts openly and boldly.

We eat breakfast standing up. I pack two liters of water under my parka and realize I look more like Santa Claus than a fit and trim mountaineer with a 3,000-foot climb ahead of him. We all tuck a half-loaf of energy-rich pound cake into our packs and set out.

We meet Dennis and his porter at the trailhead and say our goodbyes. I throw my arms around him and wish him a safe descent. I see a glimpse of relief on his face and hear the genuinely encouraging tone in his voice as he sends us on our way.

"See you guys at base camp," he says. "We'll walk down together."

Dennis watches us head up the mountain, Mike in the lead, followed by Eric, Troy, Vince, me, Jeff, and Rolo.

We spend the first part of the morning traversing through scree fields and broken rocks. There is not a lick of wind; which is amazing after what we'd endured during the past eighteen hours. I gaze at the sky and the blue is unblemished by even a single cloud. My eyes begin to well up under my goggles at the feeling in my body: these are tears of pure joy. Then I laugh out loud because I am afraid the tears will cause my eyelids to freeze shut, a very real possibility in these frigid conditions. I am also embarrassed to be crying and try to hide this from the other men.

I glance over my shoulder again. With every step, Jeff falls further and further behind us, Rolo staying with him every step of the way.

———

Jeff doesn't want us to wait on him.
He has to set his own pace.
The four of us have to set ours.

———

In life and on the mountain, it has to be that way sometimes. When you're reaching for your summit, sometimes you can't slow down, and sometimes you shouldn't slow down.

Our goals are all the same. Jeff has his priorities in order; at this point in the climb, he has to be more committed to reaching the summit than to trying to match the pace that the other four of us are setting. I couldn't respect him more for that decision. It shows leadership. It shows persistence and self-honesty.

We take a break at Independencia Hut, the highest refuge in the world. We are the first group on the mountain that day to reach Independencia, and I have to say that I take pride in that fact. We eat pound cake and drink water.

Just about the time that we are shouldering our packs again, a German man in his early sixties arrives at the hut with another guide outfit. He doesn't look good. I can see his eyes as he lifts his goggles, and he has the same look on his face that Dennis had had. It's an eerie look that says, "My brain is swollen Jell-O right now." I make a brief attempt to communicate with him, but he speaks no English. I nod and turn away, hoping he's in better shape than he looks.

The climb up from Independencia is a steady traverse that leads to a stout ridge known as Cresta del Viento, the windy ridge. From here, the views looking out over the Andes, down to Plaza de Mulas, and beyond are indescribably beautiful. The temperature is definitely a factor here, especially with the wind. I put one foot in front of the other, concentrating only on that.

Beyond the windy ridge is what is known as the Cave. We're fortunate that the traverse here is relatively gentle, because the footing is treacherous and unstable. I glance back and hope to catch a glimpse of Rolo's red jacket, but he and Jeff are well behind us now.

The Cave ends at the base of the infamous Canaleta. The Canaleta is a long, steep gully that rises nearly 1,200 feet over a frustrating mix of loose sand and gravel.

———

**It will take every ounce of strength
and a good deal of patience.
The danger level is high.**

———

Three and a half hours later, we reach a cliff face that marks the end of the Canaleta. We don't realize at the time that Jeff and Rolo had seen another climber fall almost right in front of them. It was the same German man I had seen earlier at the hut. He apparently snagged his crampon and lost his balance. Only later would we find out that he had perished in the fall. Only later would we learn what both Jeff and Rolo had had to go through, both physically and emotionally, to continue on their own journey up the mountain. In a word: surreal.

On the way up to the top of the Canaleta, we negotiate a very steep grade with our ice axes. I'm grateful for the crampons we have worn throughout most of the day. It's exceptionally hard work: a step, a breath, a moment, and then another step. One step at a time and literally climbing in Eric's footprints, we finally see the final steps to the summit.

Beyond this, a high arch of stone and snow called the Cresto del Guanaco bridges the great mountain's north and south summits. Our goal is the north summit, which is higher by only a few feet than its southern counterpart.

We trudge past a small aluminum cross, a singular marker for the highest point in the Americas.

Mike photographs the last steps of our ascent. I nod to Eric, and he is the first of our team up on the summit. I follow him up and throw my arms around him.

"We made it," he shouts in my ear.

"We did."

Troy and Vince follow, a few minutes behind, and we celebrate: four men reaching our summit on a day we will never forget. The emotions and the views we feel and see are hard to put into words. The sheer and frightening cliffs of the south face take our breath away. To the southwest, I am amazed at the sight of the mountains of Tupungato. The Horcones Inferior Glacier and Plaza Francia bleed off to the south, and the rugged, endless ranges of the Andes move well beyond our sight.

**Seeing our team on the top of
this magnificent mountain,
I realize that anything is possible.**

The Aconcagua Man Project had begun as a wistful idea ten months before and become a reality before I barely realized it.

Everything has a starting point. For us, standing here atop Aconcagua is an affirmation of what is possible for any man or woman. The attributes of success are available to all of us: commitment, accountability, and preparation. It is a question of whether or not we are willing to take ownership of those attributes.

When you stand atop a mountain—any mountain that represents your personal Aconcagua—realizing, as we were at that moment, that you've accomplished something exceptional, in company with an exceptional team, a state of unification occurs. For the Aconcagua team, we were at that moment brothers-in-arms. That was a unification that went beyond language.

It came from the depth of our being.

Tributes

Before we left for Aconcagua, Troy had designed a flag in honor of John Regan, the man who had fallen to his death on Longs Peak in Colorado the same day our team was also on that mountain. Troy had contacted John's wife about his idea for the tribute, and she shared the fact that climbing Aconcagua had also been on her husband's bucket list. The flag is Troy's way of honoring John, and

181

he unfurls it on the summit. It reads: John M. Regan –
Husband, Brother, Friend, Mountaineer.

It is a moving moment.

Then it is my turn. I unfurl a red banner with the
letters TBOLITNFL printed across it. The letters stand for
"The Best Offensive Lineman In the National Football
League." It was created by Steve Hardison, my own
mentor and coach, in tribute to Arizona Cardinal lineman
Deuce Lutui and his fascinating story of awakening,
empowerment, transformation, and the power of personal
internal commitment. If you are interested in the Deuce
Lutui story, go to www.tbolitnfl.com.

Here, at a summit representing my own internal
commitment, I am proud to be the ambassador of this
extraordinary message.

Finally, Troy and I deliver the two stuffed bears that
Greg had asked us to carry to the summit in honor of his
family, and we proudly lay them at the foot of the
aluminum cross, along with John Regan's flag and my
banner.

Then it is time to go. Our return to High Camp will
take several more hours, and I look forward to getting back
to my tent to send a message home to family and friends.
The best part of the descent is sharing water and
encouragement with Jeff and Rolo as they ascend the
summit. Five of us, out of the seven-man team that made
up the Aconcagua Man Project, reached the summit that
day. The other two had reached their summits earlier in the
climb.

Presence

I didn't know what to expect as we packed our gear at
High Camp, turned our back on the great Aconcagua's

summit, and began our descent to Base Camp at 13,800 feet, by way of the mountain's south face.

In many ways, it may have turned out to be the most important, most vibrant part of the entire experience. Climbing down the mountain, the five of us were in high spirits. What I felt was "presence," the most complete and compelling feeling of presence I had ever experienced up to that moment in my life. That was a sensation that rang out with a singular message: that life is precious beyond words.

I know how easily those words roll off the tongue. I know how many gurus of spirit and meditation preach about the importance of being present, of living in the moment, and of traveling the path of the here and now. Unfortunately, we spend far too much time theorizing about such concepts and far too little time acting on them, living them, and doing them. We read, we listen to commentary, we postulate, but we forget that the only thing that matters is being present itself.

**The descent down Aconcagua,
a day of brilliant sunshine
and powerful gusts of very cool air,
was the "experience" of presence for me,
not just the theory of it.**

I was nowhere else but in that moment. I was not back on the summit celebrating. I was not thinking about home. I was not anticipating a cold beer back at the hotel in Mendoza. I was fully within myself. I was connected with the act of being. And the lesson was powerful and binding.

You don't have to scale an impossibly difficult mountain peak to exalt in the preciousness of life. As men, we get trapped in the vicious cycle of planning, anticipating, and hypothesizing. It's almost second nature to be looking ahead or peeking in the rearview mirror. "What's next" is right up there with "Remember when?" when you look at a man's repertoire of overused phrases. How are we going to get this or get that? How are we going to impress this person or avoid that person? How can we work harder or not work at all?

**Ironically, the real work comes
in maximizing the spirit of now.**

I am not criticizing theory. Theories provide direction. Theories can even provide impetus and motivation. But for those of us who want to live extraordinary lives—and what man doesn't—all the talk about getting out of our comfort zones and stretching ourselves doesn't mean much if we don't take the action truly required to get there.

Talking about getting out of your comfort zone is just talk until you do something that makes you truly uncomfortable and that exposes your vulnerability. Then and only then can you maximize your essential value as a human being. Then and only then can you view with clarity the true value of yourself as a person and the gifts you have to offer in your relationships, in your community, and in the workplace.

Experience trumps theory every day of the week when it comes to valuing your existence. It moves your perspective. It heightens your world-view. But experience is also more risky. Experience opens a door on possible failure. Experience takes work. It means pushing yourself. It means getting up off the couch and doing what you promised that you would do.

As we hiked down the mountain that second day of February, I understood that the exceptional, remarkably clear presence of mind that I was feeling could, in part, be attributed to the fact that we had prevailed. We had overcome every obstacle the mountain had to offer. We had grown and changed minute by minute. The payoff going forward was enormous.

I knew instinctively that everything I did from that day onward would be easier and more rewarding. I would come home and experience greater levels of deep commitment in all areas of my life.

I would come home with a deeper perspective about the word commitment and how it affected everything in my life, including my ability and my willingness to say no.

I would understand that no is a perfectly valid and acceptable commitment. Knowing this, I would also understand that saying yes would have a deeper and more resonant value concerning who I am as a man.

———

**When a man understands this duality
between yes and no,
commitment takes on a whole new quality.**

———

We all have a personal "Aconcagua." Most of us have more than one. We all have a summit we're striving to reach. Yes, the seven members of the Aconcagua team were focused on climbing the great mountain itself, all with great success. But each of us, back in our homes in Colorado; now face the enviable challenge of identifying a new "Aconcagua," a new goal, a new way of pushing ourselves even closer to being the men we want to be. Mine might be business related. It might involve a personal matter. It will be up to me to determine what it is.

This is the very satisfying task that you also face: to determine what your own personal "Aconcagua" is. This is the first step.

Please note the use of the word "determine." It was not chosen at random. It derives, rather obviously, from determination, which is an essential in the pursuit of any "Aconcagua" endeavor.

Persistence, personal integrity, self-honesty, and inner commitment: these are the attributes necessary for anyone stepping into the realm of the uncomfortable. And the realm of the uncomfortable is the place where growth and change flourish.

We spent the night of February 2 at Base Camp. Dennis met us there; he looked healthy, rested, and reasonably content with his decision not to attempt the summit.

The next day, we finished our Aconcagua trek with a twenty-five-mile hike back to Penitentes, less the fifty-pound packs we'd been hauling around for sixteen days.

The route took us along the south face of Aconcagua. The view was sensational.

An even more spectacular view is the one we all have of life, and you will be amazed at how this view is immeasurably enhanced the moment you identify a personal "Aconcagua" and commit yourself to achieving it.

There will never be a better moment than right now. Take it as a personal challenge. Put a name to that one thing that you want to do going forward, that one thing that will challenge you, that one thing that will have you reaching for the summit.

The Aconcagua Man Team & Our Guides

Bottom row, left to right: (order by design) The Aconcagua Man Team: Stephen McGhee, Greg Aden, Troy Wagner, Eric Wiseman, Jeff Patterson, Dennis Carruth, Vince Ruland,

Top row, left to right: Lead guide, Mike Bradley, Vail, CO; Bolivian guide, Augusto Ortega, record holder on Aconcagua; Argentinean guide, Rolo Abaca, Rolo Denali Project

Team and guides after the last supper, before the climb.

The Aconcagua Man Team ready to put boots on the dirt.

Team Meeting, Band of Brothers, High Camp 2

Some say Aconcagua is a big rock pile. I say beauty is in the eye of the beholder. The Aconcagua Man Team doing some very careful stepping.

Stephen McGhee, with a view that took his breath away.

Jeff and Troy living it up at 19,000 feet. Nice hair boys.

High Camp 3, the night before the summit.

Troy Wagner celebrating his climb to freedom,
on the summit.

Troy & Stephen at the summit with Greg Aden's bears.

Stephen McGhee holds a flag representing
his P.I.C. (Personal Internal Commitment).
See www.TBOLITNFL.com

PART III – THE INTEGRATION

16 THE INEVITABLE SHIFT

Every significant event leads to integration.

Every time a man forges into new territory—whether it's a new adventure, a new job, or a new relationship—he experiences a shift. It is inevitable. The shift is exactly why we make ourselves uncomfortable by pushing out beyond the bounds of the world of stagnation and complacency. The shift is a natural part of every exploration, big or small, every new enterprise, and every new test of our leadership.

The integration piece of our journey represents how we deal with the shift, what we take away from the climb, and how we use it in search of the thing that we've been calling our purpose.

———

**The problem lies in identifying the shift,
and the Aconcagua Man Project
proved to be the perfect example.**

———

Identifying the shift is a deep and profound question, and one that may not be entirely answerable. For our part, I would like to report a most romantic tale of success: we all returned changed and inspired men; we all came away from the mountain filled with illumination and focus; we all came home and fulfilled, beyond our expectations, our goal of service to others.

That, unfortunately, is never the case with integration. It's not romantic and ideal. It's a reality that is more like a roller coaster.

Were there glimpses of illumination in the first weeks after our return to the States? Absolutely. Eric Wiseman came off the mountain fully committed for the first time to starting a family, and his wife Adina became pregnant not long thereafter. Eric also came away from the summit of Aconcagua with serious questions about his career. His dream of building his mountaineering company, 14er Fitness, was no longer the rock solid proposition it had seemed to be when we departed. With fatherhood comes responsibilities that many men grapple with and most embrace; Eric embraced these and made a committed return to the financial world. Battling Aconcagua's rugged slopes and reaching her precipitous 22,834-foot summit meant an extraordinary amount to Eric. It satisfied something inside him—an inner drive and an inner need—and opened the door to a more mature man. That was a shift indeed.

Dennis returned to Denver and took on a new consulting job that he hopes will free him of his entanglements in the real estate industry. At sixty-seven, this represents an opportunity for him to mentor an upcoming group of younger entrepreneurs. In turn, Dennis hopes this will be a step toward teaching and public speaking at the university level, the "service" arena that he began targeting as part of the preparation stage of the Aconcagua Man Project. Dennis has inspired college crowds such as those at the University of Wyoming with the lessons he learned on Aconcagua. I know he will continue to speak and inspire groups with his wisdom and experience.

Will this new sixty-hour-a-week commitment leave him any time to write, a long-suppressed passion? Is this consulting work a step closer to his ultimate purpose? Dennis has so much to offer to aspiring entrepreneurs, and the dogged determination that carried him through the training phase of the project, and on the climb itself, is nothing if not an exceptional example to young people of how to pursue their dreams. Will the integration phase of the project afford him the opportunity to share it? That is the question.

I know this much. Coming off the mountain, with an extraordinary feat under my belt, I expected things to be easier.

Here we've accomplished this remarkable goal, conquered the highest peak in the Americas; we did what we said we would do. On the heels of that, everything should be easier, right? Well, not so fast.

Accomplishments, regardless of size or shape, have both an upside and a downside. Doing something because you said you would do it gives you a greater sense of self, to be sure, but that comes with a hidden caveat. Now you know yourself better. Now it's harder to hide from the truth.

**Successful integration is about being
totally honest with yourself.
And a deeper sense of self leaves a man
with less room to be dishonest with himself.**

This is part of the challenge. How willing are you to be totally honest with yourself?

One of two things is going to happen. One, you are going to own this deeper sense of self. You are going to be totally honest about your life and your world. Are you really where you want to be?

Let's be clear. This is not what his wife wants his life or his world to be. This is not what his boss or his best friend wants it to be. This is one of those times when a man looks in the mirror and is willing to answer the question from the deepest part of himself. And if his life in his world isn't where he wants it to be, what can he do to make it better?

Jeff Patterson came off Aconcagua and recognized that some fundamental changes were necessary in his world. He realized there were important adjustments he needed to make in order to take his business to the next level, and he understood they would require some sacrifices. He has doubled his gross business revenue since his return. Doubled it, which is outstanding! He left for the climb in January unsettled in his relationship with his girlfriend, Lindsay, and came off the mountain knowing he wanted to build a life with her. He proposed two weeks after returning home. I personally officiated at his wedding in Aspen, Colorado this past September. It was beautiful.

200

The climb was a killer for Jeff. He was extremely uncomfortable for sixteen days, fighting headaches and nausea every step of the way; most people would have turned back. He didn't. He used the discomfort to push himself to his limits. He came home willing to do the same thing.

Greg Aden returned home from Aconcagua, the first of our group to reach his personal summit at roughly 17,000 feet, and essentially turned his long-standing priorities for life and love upside down. Career had always been at the top of Greg's list: work, advancement, and money. His commitment to society was second, followed by an emphasis on home and family. But that's no longer true. Family comes first now: his wife, his kids, and their well-being. What he can contribute to society comes in second. His career is now in third place.

Greg continues to advance in his work at IHG. He has since been promoted, which is a very interesting result, given his newfound commitment to family. He has stepped into a full-on leadership role at IHG and deepens his inspiration to himself and the teams around him. With the recent birth of his son, Brooks Campbell Aden, Greg and his wife Laura are now parents to three amazing kids, and I suspect both his company and his family appreciate the shifts Greg has gone through since returning from the mountain.

**A man owning his newfound sense of self,
and acting on it, is a good result on every level.**

The other road a man can travel down, after facing the challenges of his personal Aconcagua, is to avoid the new, irrevocable, and challenging sense of self. It's easy to do. He might very well revert back to being the man he was before the "preparation" and the "climb." Some men will stay in jobs they profess to hate. Some men will plod along in relationships that are the most unsatisfying things in the world just because the alternative is scary and uncertain.

Troy Wagner was the one member of our team who turned more inward and more introspective on the climb. In the aftermath, the shift for him turned out, as of this writing, to be less definitive, if no less important. He is still in the same job and doing his best at it, but questions remain about his love for it. Troy made an extraordinary commitment during the climb. He promised our team to lead a project called The Rolo Denali Project. The project will assist Rolo, our Argentinean guide, to help him fulfill a life-long dream of climbing Denali, the highest peak in North America and one of the Seven Summits. The Seven Summits are the highest mountains on each of the seven continents, and summiting all of them is regarded as a serious mountaineering feat.

As I write this, I am aware that I don't really know what shifted for Troy as a result of his journey up the mountain. I suspect there is a deeper sense of self for him, which has inspired him to be more of who he is. In some ways, I do believe that his experience may go beyond words, but if all he came away with from his experience was a commitment to love people more, that would be Herculean.

———

**Here's the thing. "Getting it done,"
whatever that means in your world,
is what the integration stage is all about.**

———

In the case of the Aconcagua Man Project, this means recapturing the momentum that drove us to dedicate nine months of our lives toward preparing for and reaching the summit of the mountain. For men in general, it means recapturing the momentum that drives us to undertake anything that's out of our comfort zone.

Integration requires a ton of self-honesty. And sometimes it leads you down a most unexpected road.

Returning from the slopes of Aconcagua and the remarkable high of reaching its 22,834-foot summit has not been easy for me personally. Self-honesty can be a bitch sometimes, and it came to roost right on my front porch. I came off the mountain knowing in my heart of hearts that I want to be a father. I want a family. I am not the same man who ventured onto the rocky slopes of Aconcagua in January, and this new man had to be completely honest about his feelings. The revelation was extraordinary for me, but it meant the end of a relationship I had been in for years. It meant the end of being in relationships where I cannot be fully who I really am. It meant coming to terms with my own humanity.

Several weeks later I was encouraged by my coach and mentor, Steve Hardison, to spend some time defining in my own eyes exactly what a lifetime partner would look like. I have to admit that it was with a certain sense of

203

trepidation that I took up Steve's challenge, but the result was two pages of the most honest writing I've ever done.

Here's how I opened the piece:

> *I want to find a woman who wants to get married and create a family together. To some it may seem odd that I am willing to put myself out there with such clarity and purpose in the area of romance. To me, finding that special woman to spend the rest of my life with is the single most important thing I could do. Do I feel vulnerable? Yes, and it is also a very enlivening experience.*

Honesty is risky. We all get that. But what we often miss is just how energizing and revitalizing it is. Here I am; take me or leave me. So I went on to write:

> *To me, the single most important quality I want in this partnership is God Awareness. I want to be with a conscious woman that understands the spiritual nature of love, life, and partnership. If you are for me, you are wise, loving, and appreciate the power in your feminine energy. You are a Goddess and you want to be with a man that can appreciate the true nature of your spirituality.*

I remember reading those words over and feeling the kind of strength that can only come from a place deep inside you. The willingness to do that was part of the shift I was experiencing post-climb. I have to give Steve credit for pushing me to explore it. And sometimes that's what integration takes: a push.

In addition, and after nearly twenty years of building businesses through leadership, I have decided to create a whole new distinctive type of leadership coaching. I am attracting powerful men and women leaders from across the globe to re-define their own brand of leadership and apply it to a greater good for the world. I am playing a bigger game.

Self-honesty requires courage. It required courage for me to put my ass out on the line in my work and to engage clients that require me to show up one hundred percent every single day.

Self-honesty is never comfortable. Coming to terms with where you are in your life and where you want to be is dicey. And sometimes it's hard to remember that real personal growth comes most readily from putting yourself in a position of feeling uncomfortable.

Leadership requires tremendous integration of events that have taken place in the past.

———

**If you choose to ignore those events,
you can rest assured they will bite
you in the ass again one day.
If you can embrace them, you will evolve
into a more conscious human being.**

———

Some men don't see that pushing the envelope in terms of the world they're living in is the only way to rise above mediocrity and the status quo.

It may be easier to put in your hours at a job that isn't particularly satisfying, but what do you have when it comes down to measuring the quality of your life?

Here is the beauty of honesty. It allows each of us, as men, to serve the causes that are most important to us at the deepest level, whether it's being a father or a philanthropist, an artist or a mentor, a businessman or bricklayer. It allows us to serve our ongoing relationships without apology and to build new relationships with integrity. It allows us to see when the ship that is our lives is floundering and set it right with courage.

A large measure of our success as men comes from service. You've felt it. I've felt it. Service taps a place deep inside us. It's that feeling that says, "Yes, this is why I was put on this earth." Service is made clearer and more intimate when as men we flat out refuse to be dishonest with ourselves. Easy? Not on your life. Worthwhile? Think about it: is there anything more worthwhile?

Here's the challenge. As men, we're dealing with a stacked deck. Society has created this insufferable mold that you and I are supposed to conform to, but integration is about living and loving from our own point of view, not society's.

Coming off Aconcagua, after punching my way to the summit and realizing the culmination of nine months of preparation and planning, I felt as if I'd experienced something almost greater than intimacy.

This is what I wrote to a friend during our last night on the mountain:

> *I uncorked it. As a man, I went to the deepest, most residual places of my fear and faced them. I faced my own death and knew of another man that plummeted to his death on our summit day. I am free now. I am open, loving, and relaxed to be all that God would have me be. I can't really explain it. I am no*

longer chasing anything. I am no longer worried about what others think. I am on the other side of things. I have attempted my summit through the University of Santa Monica (amazing program www.gousm.edu), Insight, Landmark, Relationships, Fasting, and Retreats and all the while knew there was something that had a hold on me. Aconcagua took a scalpel to my consciousness and released me of my self-imposed restrictions. The mountain kicked my ass and my fear out of me. She (Aconcagua) is the ultimate woman. She fucked me open in my fear and put my heart in my head.

What did this all mean once I got on a plane knowing that I had a business to run the minute I hit the ground, a business I had put on hold for three weeks? What did this all mean, knowing that so many people had been cheering on our efforts and how important the project had become to them? How do you explain the amorphous shift you know has occurred?

There were a number of things I couldn't put my finger on, though they were easy to express. I knew that I had returned home with a deeper calm, a deeper self-knowing, a deeper sense of peace: amazing gifts that were apparent to most of my closest friends and even to some newer acquaintances. One woman called it "a surfer's secret."

I didn't get it at first. And then it began to dawn on me that the shift I was experiencing was toward simplicity. My view of the world was simpler: more powerful, to be sure, but also simpler. What did this mean? It came back to the point of greater honesty. If there is no equivocation in your thinking, then there will be no room for evasiveness In your actions.

We are a society built upon lies. We spend most of our time lying to ourselves about the direction of our lives and what we're trying to accomplish, and we've gotten so good at it that living the lie seems normal. Many of us are in jobs we don't like. Some of us ignore our passions, because we're convinced we don't have the time or the money to indulge in them. We go to parties, get loaded, and need to be loaded to have fun. We forget about the simple things that bring us joy. We push aside our dreams and aspirations and replace them with wishful thinking.

What often happens then is that seeking the truth—which should be at the top of our list—takes a back seat to getting through the day unscathed. This is when the shift that we experience in the accomplishment of any endeavor, whether climbing a mountain in Argentina or creating a new work of art in our basement studio, gets lost.

17 BEING MAN

The latest and greatest product on the shelves of evolutionary remedies is going to be what I call "beingness."

We can define beingness in a number of ways. We could call it existing in the moment. We could call it the state of actuality. We could call it being alive. You get the picture. It's one of those ambiguous terms that is often dismissed, in particular by men, as sounding too New Age-y or too metrosexual. It's neither.

Here is the question we all have to ask, whether we're a biker riding our Harley Davidson to a rally in South Dakota or a Mr. Mom staying at home with the kids and home-schooling them. It doesn't matter if you're a lawyer, a construction worker, or a venture capitalist. Are you "being" a person of complete self-honesty when you look in the mirror and ask, "Am I really "being" the kind of man I want to be, or am I playing a part designed by all the pressures of society? Am I doing all I can do to chase down my dreams, or have I fallen into the trap of trying to satisfy the expectations of everyone but me?"

That's getting us closer to an understanding of "beingness."

———

**The man you are being today will dictate
the man you will become tomorrow.**

———

The word honest is derived from the Latin pia pium , meaning "being" one with what is. This might very well translate into being more honest with your wife about your sex life, rather than spending all your sexual energy exploring porn sites on the internet. It might translate into being honest with your boss when he's behaving like an asshole and bringing down the whole team. The bottom line is that if you cannot be honest with yourself, then there is no way you will be honest with others.

———

**We all have the impulse toward self-honesty:
the impulse to be open and forthcoming.**

———

Unfortunately, we've been wired to think that we lose our negotiating advantage if we're too honest. We've been taught that a white lie is better than taking the risk of hurting someone's feelings. We've discovered that there's safety in sitting on the fence. What often gets lost in the mix of this ambiguous thinking is how easy it becomes to lie to ourselves.

It's a conundrum. The last thing we want to do is deceive our inner being, but we live in a world where that deception is a powerful force.

A question that exposes a man's core is, "Who am I being today, right now, in this moment?" Perhaps you're sitting in a business meeting playing the role of a business owner or salesman or engineer, and the rules of engagement dictate you adopt a certain sort of decorum to fit the occasion and a certain political correctness to satisfy the pecking order. We've all been in meetings with our own agenda, and we're often willing to sacrifice a sliver of our integrity to get what we want. We may not even know that we're doing it.

Do you leave the meeting feeling authentic, or do you leave the meeting feeling like a fraud? Either way, your "beingness" is at stake. If you leave the meeting feeling authentic, your "being" is intact; you're solidifying who you are as a person and a man. If you don't—if you even slightly compromise your values—you're leaking your core self.

**The thing about this is that it's tough
to stop the leaking once it's started.**

With this in mind, let's turn the spotlight back on the Aconcagua Man Project. From the beginning, it was almost impossible for the team to hide from itself. Part of the commitment each of us made when we signed on to the project in May of 2010 was genuine openness about where we were in our lives, and more than that, where we wanted to be in our lives going forward.

The team did more than train together; we built a substantial level of trust, and that trust allowed Jeff to talk candidly about his world in a small mountain town, Eric to

211

confide in matters close to his heart, and Dennis to open up about his business concerns. At the time, Troy was going through a difficult divorce, Greg was adopting a baby and learning to be a step-father, and Vince was trying to justify leaving the country for three weeks when he had business and personal matters looming on the horizon. My goal was to share my thoughts about dynamic leadership without infringing on the collaborative model the project was meant to develop.

We built an atmosphere where "beingness" felt almost natural, even if it was uncomfortable. The level of self-honesty was empowering, even if it was uncomfortable. But that was the whole point; feeling uncomfortable meant we were exploring new ground. The challenge came when we put away our training gear and returned home and back to the workplace. Would we be able to maintain that sense of "beingness" in those settings?

But it was more than that. When you commit yourself to something outside your comfort zone, you're exposed. Good or bad, the real "you" has to shine through, and that's probably the very best argument I can make for pursuing your own personal Aconcagua, whether it's that African safari you've always dreamed about or relocating your office in a small town far from the hustle and bustle of the city. You're stretched. You're uncomfortable. You're growing. When change is happening all around you, it's hard not to be authentic. And that's what six months of hard training and personal honesty did for the Aconcagua team.

Here's another point that bridges the training work we put in preparing for our climb and the climb itself.

**Beingness—this point of self-honesty,
authenticity, and integrity—
is also tied directly to accountability.**

As overworked as the term "accountability" is in some arenas, a man willing to be clear about where he is in his life will never be anything less than accountable. He will never be anything less than responsible. He knows that if he chooses, even once, not to be answerable for his actions, he begins to leak the essence of his inner being.

You can't fake it. I speak from experience. You can't fake accountability. You either are, or you're not. You can't fake responsibility. And you can't fake this ambiguous thing we're calling "beingness."

I can tell you one thing without a moment's hesitation. On the climb up Aconcagua itself, three miles and more above sea level, there is no place to hide. There is also no one to impress. When you're on a mountain for sixteen days, where all your focus is on putting one foot in front of the other one, with fifty pounds strapped to your back, it's hard to be anyone other than the authentic you.

**The challenge is to bring that authentic self
back with you and to integrate it successfully
into your day-to-day life.**

The challenge for us was not to let the shift we'd experienced get buried under the weight of responsibilities

213

that looked pretty much the same way they did before we left for Argentina. The challenge for us was to hold onto the shift, even in our relationships with people who hadn't been privy to our "Aconcagua" moment.

If beingness leads to becoming, the question each of us had to ask, coming off Aconcagua, was, "Who have I become?" The answer lies in our willingness to be totally honest with ourselves, and that is always the rub. What if the answer isn't pleasant? What if who I have become doesn't fit my current relationships and the responsibilities? Then what? Am I willing to be honest enough to make them fit in accordance with the newly-discovered me? Am I honest enough to say, for example, "This doesn't work for me anymore," ending, as I did, a relationship with a woman I was deeply in love with?

**Society tells us that we can fake
self-honesty up to a degree.
It's almost considered a murky art form.**

I'm lucky. I happen to be in a profession where any shred of dishonesty on my part sticks out like a sore thumb. I'm held accountable because of the nature of my relationships with my clients and the interpersonal way I do business. Not everyone is as lucky.

The perfect meld between self-honesty and personal integrity is what provides the fortification of spirit and self. The velocity that propels a person into living his or her life the very best way possible comes from a place deep inside. It cannot come from any place else. We know that instinctively. We know, for example, that the velocity

214

doesn't come from having material wealth or the acquiring of material things. It's not propelled by position.

Material wealth and position cannot hide the fact that you're either honest or dishonest with yourself and with others; neither material wealth nor position can hide the fact that you're either holding firm to your inner being or you're leaking it. It always comes back around to a single question. What is your truth?

Taking the magic of your Aconcagua, whatever that might be, and integrating it into your world doesn't come with any deliverance from all of the idiosyncrasies that accompany being a human being. You still have to get up in the morning, brush your teeth, and fix breakfast. You still have to find your way in the world. Successful integration just means you're doing it on your own terms.

Dennis came back from Argentina after reaching his personal summit at high camp, an altitude of 19,200 feet; an amazing accomplishment. He had inferred, as the climb progressed, that reaching High Camp would fulfill his Aconcagua. It proved to be a self-fulfilling prophecy. He felt strong for the better part of the climb, but a cautionary voice told him that High Camp was high enough.

Dennis had spoken often, during the nine months that we prepared for our climb, about his desire to expand his service efforts when he returned from Argentina. In a perfect world, he would exit the real estate business for a more service-based pasture. Instead, he came home and took a well-paid position with a company in Denver, a very long way from his home in Aspen. He did it for the money, but he also did it because he felt that he could mentor the company's management group. Was this a compromise to his real aspirations for post-climb integration or a step in the right direction? Only Dennis knows the answer.

———

At some point, we all have to find the one thing that we love and adjust our lives accordingly. This goes to the issue of a deeper sense of self and self-honesty.

———

I used Dennis as an example because we all looked to him for his unique brand of wisdom during the preparation and climb phases of the project, and we will continue to do that for a long while, post-climb.

But as I said in Part II of the book: No new behavior shows up on the mountain. You can't say you'll be happy making it as far as High Camp and then expect to make it to the summit.

You can reword this statement to fit any project that you undertake or any new relationship that you pursue. I love this quote by Michel de Montaigne that sums up the dilemma. "The great and glorious masterpiece of man is to know how to live to purpose." This is easier said than done, but what better goal could we have?

The greatest challenge of the integration phase of any worthwhile endeavor is nudging yourself toward new behavior. You have to do it. That's what growth is. That's what evolution is. And if you're growing and evolving, then you're integrating the shift that every "Aconcagua" endeavor creates.

This circle of growth and evolution begins with "beingness," which is the first step to becoming. It's up to us to determine what that means.

18 VULNERABILITY: A STRENGTH, NOT A WEAKNESS

What is it that holds us back?

What is it that keeps us from that one pursuit, that one thing that we really want to be doing? That one adventure we've always dreamed of. That one endeavor which always seems to get pushed to the back burner. That one business idea we've been nurturing for a decade or more.

The question of what holds us back is cause for deep introspection. And the deepest, most conflicting reason that you, I, or anyone else decides against going for that adventure, endeavor, or dream; that "one thing," is rationalization.

The short definition of rationalization is a "rational lie." It's a defense mechanism, and one that every person in the world uses at one point or another. A good, old-fashioned rationalization comes in multifarious forms. The two most potent and overworked forms center on time and money, as in "I don't have the time," or "I don't have the money."

217

How many times have we heard someone say, "It won't work. Why waste the energy," or "I can't do it," or "It won't matter anyway." I always like it when someone deflects the blame from his or her self with something like, "I can't. I have a family," or "My wife would go through the roof if I even mentioned it."

Why do we rationalize?
The most obvious explanation is fear.

We're afraid: afraid of failing, afraid of disappointment, or afraid of not living up to our own expectations.

Rationalization is a killer when it comes to effective integration. The willingness to make excuses regarding our intentions or our actions is a direct conduit for fooling and flat-out being dishonest with ourselves. It makes it impossible to embrace the shift that comes with the integration phase of any important endeavor.

How often do we conceal our true feelings or our true motivations in the face of stress and insecurity? Instead, we tell a small lie or manufacture a plausible excuse. Instead, we return to the status quo and accept the road to mediocrity.

Fear is an innate instinct. We were born with fear's self-protection mechanism built into us. But too often, we view fear as that thing which holds us back. In fact, fear can be used to move a person forward.

**A fear overcome is a stepping-stone into the unknown,
and it is our explorations into the unknown or
the untried that stimulate growth and provide
acceleration toward change.**

I have a client who most of us would view as a successful businessman, but his primary fear lies in the area of vulnerability. He masks this fear by maintaining an air of confrontation and resistance. Despite his financial successes, it will be impossible for him to integrate the positive aspects of his life as long as this conflict rules his behavior. His task, while working with me, is to identify his vulnerability and turn it into a strong suit.

**You cannot achieve or accomplish anything great or
significant without allowing yourself to be vulnerable.
Vulnerability isn't a show of weakness;
it's a show of strength.**

You can bet that climbing Aconcagua required a huge admission of vulnerability. A mountain soaring nearly 23,000 feet above sea level is just waiting to kick your butt, and if you're not willing to admit the possibility of this and the absolute assurance of enduring some serious suffering, you should turn around at Mendoza and head home. Otherwise, you're asking for trouble.

What happened to my good friend Greg Aden at 16,300 feet, when he officially announced to the rest of the team his decision to return to Mendoza and a plane ride home?

He seemed clear and resolute in his decision, but I wonder if there wasn't another side to his decision to call Camp 1 his summit, which was a struggle with the issue of vulnerability that we're discussing.

Jeff tried to point something out to Greg the morning of his announcement. What Jeff said was, "Greg, you're the guy we all count on to have it together. You're the guy that everyone back home counts on to have it together. You always do. You always have. But right now, maybe you don't. And you don't have to have it together. You're not feeling really great. You didn't sleep worth a damn last night. You're not climbing real strongly. We all get it. That's what this team is all about. Why don't you allow yourself to feel vulnerable and let the rest of us take up the slack for a few days until you're back on top of things?"

"I'm clear on this," he said, which we all respected. "I'm going down."

I look back on that moment now and firmly believe that Greg missed out on a seminal moment then: a moment of deep self-honesty, a moment to acknowledge his vulnerability, and a moment to look past the rationalization and the fear. A very big part of me wishes he had taken a step back then and said, "Okay, I'll take a look at what you're saying, Jeff. I'll give it some thought. Maybe you're right."

This is not to say that Greg wouldn't have gone down the mountain anyway, nor is this meant, in any way, to disrespect his decision. Greg is not that different from most men. The truth is most of us have a hard time owning up to fear and vulnerability. It seems counter-intuitive to the way most of us were brought up. Most of us see it as a show of weakness. It's not. It's an opportunity to dig deeper and come out on the other side a stronger, more open man.

―――――

**We all face "break-through" moments,
as I like to call them.
These are those moments when self-honesty
knocks on the door.**

―――――

We either grab it for all it's worth and come away from it with our integrity fully intact, or we let the moment slip past us, turn a blind eye to the opportunity, and go on our merry way.

The first of these possibilities is where integration takes on real color, and the shift becomes a viable part of your day-to-day living. The other is when we waste the fruits of our climb—whatever that climb looks like in your world—and allow the status quo to gobble us up.

Surely, I have given up on myself many times in my life. But as men, as good friends, in particular, if we hold each other accountable to our greater selves, we grow as human beings. Being held accountable, we become better human beings. The world becomes a better place. And ultimately, and most importantly, who we are "being" is fortified.

What is this concept of being fortified? This is when we are strengthened inwardly, at the core of our being, in a place where confidence and resolve meld with a sense of inner peace.

When you're "fortified," you're not looking outside yourself to be loved. You're not looking outside yourself for acceptance or approval.

Most of us do just the opposite. We look elsewhere to be loved. We look to other people for acceptance and approval. And this is where the element of fear comes into play in our lives. Who doesn't want to be loved, accepted, and approved of? But when we seek these things out of fear, rather than as a means of feeling whole or complete, the fortification of our being is what suffers.

When we returned from our climb of Aconcagua, it was not surprising that all seven of us faced crossroads with majorly life-altering prospects. This was not coincidence. This was because we'd punched a hole in the question of exactly what kind of men we wanted to be. That is what an "Aconcagua" endeavor produces. You can't pursue a personal "Aconcagua" without causing an internal shift. It's inevitable. That's why we do it.

We've talked about some of these already: Eric deciding to become a father and returning to the coat-and-tie financial world that had been so unappealing to him before the climb; Greg's very conscious decision to put his family ahead of his career; and the aggressive and perhaps overdue adjustments Jeff decided to make to his business model.

Vince Ruland, a longtime mountaineer, returned home after summiting Aconcagua with significant satisfaction and the knowledge that he no longer felt driven to climb the six other peaks of the Seven Summits (the highest peaks on each of the seven continents). No, he was not done with mountaineering by any means, but now he was driven more by the camaraderie of the sport than by the notches on his belt.

He also came home with an open heart and a desire to commit more fully to his new relationship with his girlfriend Sally. He would give one hundred percent to his project manager position at Raytheon, as he had always done, but he was even more committed to insuring that his two daughters weren't unnecessary casualties of his recent divorce. He would see them at every opportunity. He would be totally honest with them. He would be a father first.

Troy Wagner came home from Aconcagua and fell into an old trap. He pulled away from the team, failed in his commitments to his Prosperity Master Mind Team, and allowed the "silent killer" to consume him. Then he made a comeback. He explains it here in two letters sent on June 2 to the Aconcagua team and his Prosperity Team. He titled the letters *Knock Knock - Learnings from Troy Over the Past Four Months.*

This is what he wrote to us:

Dear Friends:

Can I be a member of the team again? I say this with some jest but mostly with the acknowledgement that I have pulled myself away from the team and our friendships. I think the best way for me to communicate where I've been and what I've learned is to share with you an email I sent to the Prosperity Master Mind Team.

223

All that's written below pertains to my recent interactions with this team. Besides my learning's [sic] the most important thing I'd like to say is that I'm sorry. I'm sorry I've taken our friendships for granted.

I hope you can forgive me and know that I will be an active, vulnerable and loving participant in this team.

We still have to get Rolo to Denali, a commitment that I am going to follow through on. I'm trying to realize that this is all for my highest good. My resolve is certainly being tested but I will reach that summit again.

Thanks for listening. You guys are truly a blessing to me. Much love and respect to each of you! Troy

This is what Troy wrote to his Prosperity Master Mind Team:

Dear Team:

...I'm writing this note to apologize, to share some challenges of late, associated learnings, and actions I'm taking to grow from this experience.

I feel I'm on the verge of a breakthrough but my resolve is certainly being challenged. More so than I've ever experienced. I would like to apologize for not being an active, vulnerable, and open participant in this program.

It's a growing spurt in preparation for something bigger... This is my perceived reality that I'm choosing to learn from. Live based on 'love' not fear. There is so much more power to create in 'Love.' So what does this mean to me? I need to 'Love' myself to create everything I want. That means putting 'My Purpose' as the highest priority in my life. To make it a more tangible 'My Purpose' is to follow through on my commitments. I'm choosing to live by my word. No more living based on whatever I feel like or which way the wind blows. There is so much personal value gained when you do what you say. No matter how comfortable or uncomfortable you feel about doing it. So again, I apologize for not following through on my commitment to this team...

Live in 'Love.' Prosperity Abound. Troy

Suffice it to say that integration is not always easy, and it certainly is not without some pain and struggles. Troy perceived the shift. Now will he be able to fortify the purpose that he spoke of and push forward with his many commitments? Can he drag the updated Troy out and eschew the need for acceptance and approval from outside forces? I know he means it when he says, "Live in Love." He has that capacity. And that's a powerful start.

As mentioned previously, my mentor and personal coach is a Phoenix resident named Steve Hardison. Steve may be the most fortified man I know. He has the inner strength of a giant and doesn't care a bit what anyone thinks of him or his way in the world, except for his wife Amy. The result is a man who shows up in the world as

225

powerful and confident. Steve strives for respectability, not likeability. He is not living his life to be liked, but to make a difference.

In Ralph Waldo Emerson's essay on Self-Reliance, he writes: *Speak what is true for you, and it will almost always resonate in others.*

A fortified man believes this without equivocation. Think of the power in that statement. Just speak the truth. Be totally self-honest. And what you will then find is that your views will be respected and taken as completely genuine. When you're genuine, you spend a lot less time filtering through what you should or should not say. When you're genuine, you spend a lot less time worrying about how to be loved or liked. When you're fortified, you don't have to.

Mike Bradley, our head guide on our Aconcagua expedition, is, in my eyes, an example of a man fortified to the core of his being. His willingness to be vulnerable is as apparent as the strength of character that he demonstrates. His willingness to be strong and courageous is as apparent as the forthright way in which he communicates.

A man of few words, he shared with our team the demise of his relationship with the woman he loved and cherished. This happened via a long-distance phone call the night before we were to set out on our climb. He cried like a baby. He made no attempt to hide the pain he was feeling. In my eyes, his extraordinary display of honesty told me that our team was in good hands. "Here's where I'm at. You guys need to know, because it might take me a day or so to get myself right." From my viewpoint, Mike could probably kick the crap out of any man stupid enough to be stoic in that moment.

His honesty allowed the Aconcagua team to reach out in support and do so without embarrassment. No one freaked out. No one said, "How is the guy going to give us a one hundred percent effort toward climbing over some of the roughest terrain on the planet."

That was a "break-through" moment for Mike. He put his emotions on the line and trusted seven guys he'd never met before to throw in with him, lock, stock, and barrel. We did. The message was clear. "We've got your back, Mike."

What I saw was profound. A day into our three-day trek to Base Camp, over a stretch of spectacular high-desert terrain, Mike was fully engaged again and as rock solid and focused as he could be. He was fully on purpose. Our confidence in him was, at that point, unquestionably, one hundred percent soundly, fortified.

19 NO MATTER THE QUESTION, THE ANSWER IS LOVE

I want to begin this chapter with an admonishment that I share with clients whenever I hear them say, "I should…"

"I should think about looking for that new job."

"I should just pack up my gear and head to Italy for a month. I've been promising myself that for years."

"I should really get myself in shape."

My response to this, in every case, is, "Don't 'should' on yourself."

You can think of myriad examples of "I should" situations. You've heard them come from the mouths of friends, family, colleagues, and complete strangers. It's ironic that when we hear someone else say it, we realize how impotent and demonizing it sounds.

It's no accident that "Don't 'should' on yourself" is a direct play on the words "Don't shit on yourself." They're essentially interchangeable.

Both statements are demeaning and derogatory. Both are emasculating. And perhaps more than anything, an "I should" statement lacks the kind of positive, honest energy that we've been talking about throughout this section, the kind of positive energy that solidifies the integration phase of any Aconcagua endeavor.

You can't be fortified if you're raining down on yourself with "I should" comments. "I should," "I could," "I would." They're all the same. There is no self-honesty in those comments. And there's no self-love either.

Here is one thing I know without reservation, hesitation, or equivocation. No matter what the question, the answer is always love.

A fortified man will choose love every time. Sometimes it's a tough love, no doubt about it. Sometimes it's a pragmatic love. Sometimes it's gentle and caring. Sometimes it's solicitous and inviting. Sometimes it's direct. But it is always honest. It is always from the heart.

Love, when all is said and done, is having someone else's best interest at heart. That is the guiding light.

In my hometown of Denver, much like many other big cities, there are a lot of homeless people. The street corners

230

along many main thoroughfares are populated with individuals holding handwritten, cardboard signs soliciting for money with any number of different pleas. I was in my car one morning and came to a stop across from a young woman holding a sign that read: *Can you help? 19-month-old baby. Homeless.*

Well, that's the kind of heart-wrenching commentary that is impossible for me to ignore. I stopped. I looked her straight in the eye and said, "Are you being straight with me? Do you really have a nineteen-month-old baby? And where's the father?"

She averted her eyes and said, "He's with the baby at the shelter downtown."

I believed her. At least, I wanted to believe her. I gave her twenty dollars and my phone number. I said, "When you get back to the shelter, call me and I'll help you and your husband find jobs." It wasn't an empty promise. I knew I had the resources to do that. I really hoped she would call, but I wasn't surprised when she didn't. In retrospect, I had to question myself. Had I really served her by giving her the money? I didn't regret it, but I'm not sure it was a loving thing to do: a thing that might have made a difference in the long run.

Would I have served her better by taking her hand, squeezing it firmly, and saying, "You're not a victim. Get yourself together." Would that have been worth more than twenty dollars? Would that have been a more loving thing to do?

That is a question all men have to ask themselves. What does love look like?

Love is not an emotion.
Love is a behavior.

Love is how you choose to act in the world. Love is how you choose to represent yourself in the world. When there is truth in your behavior and truth in the actions you take, then the manifestation is love.

Impulse

This is not "impulsive" behavior I'm talking about here. An impulse is the influence of a particular feeling, as in, "This is a feeling I have to follow." An impulse is an inclination that prompts us to take an action. No, it's not well thought out. It's a belief worth following that hits at a moment's notice.

Following an impulse is not a random, hit-or-miss thing. Impulses are almost always backed with truth.

Here's an example. Some years ago, I facilitated a leadership program focused on heartfelt awareness. An hour into the first day, we pushed all the chairs aside and called for the people to mingle. The explicit question they had to answer during their interaction with each person was, in effect, "What do you see in this person you're interacting with?" What characteristics did they demonstrate? What personality traits did they exhibit? In most cases, the participants had less than thirty seconds to make their analysis, which meant they were acting completely on impulse. The results, astonishingly, were consistently ninety to one hundred percent accurate.

People trusting their impulses; that's all it was.

**Impulses don't allow us to deny self-honesty.
We know, if only we will allow ourselves to know.**

———

Self-honesty and the fortification of that self-honesty was exactly what the Aconcagua Man Project was all about when we began on day one in the spring of 2010 and is what it continues to be about as we move forward during this remarkably empowering stage we call integration.

We are men, and the fortification of our belief in ourselves is what the world needs right now. The world, with all due respect to the fallacies of political correctness, does not need more nice guys who want more than anything to be liked. I'm sorry, but likeability is not the answer: respectability is the answer; inspiration is the answer.

———

The world needs men who garner our respect. The world needs men who inspire us, men who get things done, and men who don't sugarcoat the truth.

———

No, I'm not suggesting a world where people don't honor each other. I want to be honored by my friends. Of course, I do. But I also know that my friends will think more highly of me if they see a man they respect, a man who is true to his word, and a man who doesn't need their approval.

Getting Things Done

Now let's suppose that you've climbed your own personal "Aconcagua". Now you've succeeded in meeting that goal that you've set for yourself. You've made, for example, that career change. You've moved your family from Reno to Rio in pursuit of cultural bonanza. Whatever the endeavor was that you prepared for, fought for, pursued, and achieved.

Now you want to integrate the ramifications of this achievement into your fuller life. It begins with an understanding of the shift we discussed earlier. You cannot take a step forward, as our team did during our climb up Aconcagua, by precipitating a change in your consciousness. It would be impossible to experience anything like that without knocking yourself off-center in a positive way. This holds true for the pursuit of any significant endeavor.

First, you have to accept the inevitability of the shift. Secondly, you have to identify the evolution. What changed for you?

I came back from our climb knowing, without any doubt, that I wanted to create a family. This led to the end of one relationship and opened my eyes to exactly the kind of relationship I wanted with a woman.

I came down knowing that I wanted to use my business and all the relationships I had built over the years to affect a bigger picture, above and beyond my immediate impact on the individual clients I worked with. I was clear that my work in the area of leadership would be directed toward impacting global change. I made commitments to coaching leaders who were willing to produce value to the world from a deeply integral point of view.

If a door opens, you have to be willing to step past it.

One thing I discovered about the integration phase of the "Aconcagua" experience is that you have to sit with this shift. You have to meditate upon it. And then, you have to respect it.

If you don't accept this shift, and if you don't respect it, the odds of plunging back into the man you were pre-Aconcagua are almost insurmountable. As men, we cannot let this happen. The shift is too important. It signals yet another step toward becoming the man you want to be: a man of purpose, a man of significance, and a man of service.

As men, we have too much to get done. You don't come back from an "Aconcagua" experience just to sit on your rear end. You come back with things to do, and the integration phase is about doing them.

Meditation

The truth is this: our sixteen-day ascent of the immensely beautiful, immensely rugged slopes of the highest peak outside of Asia was, without question, one very long meditation. You cannot endure such an expedition without complete and total focus. The climb is all there is. Focus, purpose, and concentration: one foot in front of the other; one very long meditation.

What, you ask, does that have to do with integration? What does it have to do with getting things done?

Here at home, I meditate every morning for upwards of an hour each day. And every day, when I finish that

235

session, there is an impulse to do something constructive. I am galvanized. I'm energized. I see that "something," and I do it. I act upon that impulse. That's the power of meditation for me. It sets me in motion.

The point here is that taking action or going out in the world and integrating what you've learned or discovered from any "Aconcagua" endeavor or enterprise is steeped in self-honesty.

———

This self-honesty leads to clarity of thinking, and this is the root of the impulses that we, as men, act on.

———

Yes, meditation is, for me, one road to clarity. For you, there might be other roads. You might think more clearly while exercising. You might connect with your impulses while working in the garden. You might be deep into a project at work when the impulse hits.

Wherever or whenever these impulses hit, they are almost always based in truth. It is imperative to act on them. Too many of us don't.

———

Too many men filter their impulses based upon a desire to be liked and accepted.

———

It's a dangerous trap, because acting on impulse is a vital part of integration. It is a vital part of recognizing the shift that comes with an "Aconcagua" moment.

Earlier we said, "The answer is always love." Loving yourself enough to believe in the impulses that move you to act is a powerful thing. Too many people shrug off their impulses to act out of fear or a lack of confidence or laziness. And those three reoccurring obstacles are like nails in the coffin for a man in search of himself and his purpose.

I challenge you to think about the impulses that you've had in your life and to examine the results. I would be willing to bet that something good—maybe even something great—came from those actions. There is almost always a payoff: a sense of satisfaction, an opportunity for growth, a moment of joy, a feeling of happiness, or a new way of thinking.

A very simple example occurred for me in a coaching session today. I was on the phone with a client talking about the challenges of his growing business when I was struck with the impulse, more or less out of the blue, to say, "I have a feeling that you've had a lot of conflict in your life. Is that accurate?" He wasn't offended or taken aback. In fact, he readily admitted how true that was. A second impulse led me to make a second inquiry, "Okay, then how do you feel about being vulnerable as a man?" Wow! A door opened. Suddenly, we had a new and very vital piece to add to our discussion about his business and his approach to business.

It was a breakthrough moment based on an impulse that I followed and that he was receptive to. He was receptive to it because the root of my questions and the impulse that drove me to ask them was based completely around his well-being. They were fully grounded in the defining point of this chapter: *The answer is always love.*

How, when all is said and done, do you act with love in your heart without qualifying your beliefs or denigrating yourself as a man?

You do it with truth and self-honesty.

The Reflection in the Mirror

We've all had occasions of being dishonest with ourselves. I have had many occasions. A good part of my past was spent in the fog of what could be called "self-dishonesty."

There is not one among us who couldn't look in the mirror and own up to occasions when we did things that were not true to the person we truly wanted to be. Not with ill intent, for the most part, not at all. Most moments of self-dishonesty are moored in a desire to please someone or to be liked by someone or for purposes of advancement on one level or another.

Some might call it human nature. Actually, I think it is in our nature to be self-honest. I think a life of integrity is our true nature. But we let society beat it out of us. We get caught in the "shoulds," "coulds," and "woulds" of life. We settle, because sometimes that's easier than standing up in the face of criticism or acrimony.

And while love is always the answer, it is monumentally important for each of us as men to ask this question: when have I given up on myself to be liked or accepted by someone else?

This is a very tricky business, but you can't have it both ways.

238

You can't truly love yourself as a man and a person if you're not living with self-honesty.

The fortified man works from his core of self-honesty and truth. It's an extraordinary place to be, because it makes looking at the world in a loving, caring way so much easier. Strength of character does that.

Look at the most powerful relationships that you have. The "foxhole" friendships, if you will. The people you care enough about to be there for through thick and thin; people who will be there for you until the end. There are no veneers. These are relationships grounded in self-honesty. These are the relationships that encourage your vulnerability, and that see vulnerability as a powerful and accepted force. These are relationships where love is, indeed, the answer.

You may have friends that go back many years. But time is not the test of a foxhole friend. The litmus test of a foxhole friend is this: does he or she do what they say they are going to do, without equivocation? Is this person going to watch your back without equivocation, no questions asked?

These are relationships that are built from a foundation of truth.

I built the Aconcagua team that way. I ended up with seven men realizing that if they started with the truth—about themselves, their lives, their trials and tribulations, their fears, their successes, and their hopes—that the foundation of those relationships was going to be unshakable.

239

We made commitments along the way about service and the community and about coming away from the climb with a renewed sense of purpose about who we were as men and working toward a committed integration once we were off the mountain.

The integration phase is the most difficult, because you're no longer training as a team, and you're no longer climbing as a team. There is no place to hide in the integration of an "Aconcagua" endeavor. The team can encourage you and be there for support and counsel, but in many ways, you're on your own. You have to build new teams. You have to acknowledge your own shift. You have to fortify your own core.

It begins with an unshakeable premise: love is always the answer.

20 CULTURAL INTEGRATION

Seven men from Colorado commit themselves to an extraordinary undertaking. Our commitment is to train and prepare for a sixteen-day ascent of Aconcagua, the highest peak in the world outside of Asia. Our commitment is to support one another over the course of that climb and to return with aspirations to use what we have learned about ourselves in some manner of service toward the planet.

When we return, the seven of us will all experience something very similar as we integrate back into our worlds at home. This similarity of experience is based upon the fact that all of us come from like backgrounds. We all live in Colorado, which has its own cultural personality that is distinct from the rest of the United States. We all work, for the most part, in environments touched by the business world. Jeff and I are executive coaches working with people in a myriad of industries. Troy and Vince work for Level 3 and Raytheon respectively and are immersed in corporate America. Eric has roots in the financial community. Greg and Dennis are executives with ties to the hotel industry and to real estate.

**These may all be different occupations,
but they are not terribly disparate
when it comes to their cultural implications.**

The seven of us all live relatively comfortable existences, especially when compared with some parts of agrarian Argentina. If can also be said that we all live relatively complicated lives in comparison with that part of world.

The point here is that the Aconcagua team spent time in a part of the world that is considerably different from our own and viewed it from the perspective of American males. Our cultural point of view traveled with us to Aconcagua and returned with us as well.

**This cultural point of view colors the integration
phase, whether we acknowledge it or not.
These are the elements of integration that are
endemic to the experience in both
positive and negative ways.**

Imagine that you were a football player and your team won the Super Bowl. Rest assured that there would be attached feelings and emotions that would carry over for months and probably even years. Your interaction with people would be affected. Your job would be affected. Your view of yourself would be altered. Good or bad, these elements are inevitable. It's cultural.

In the case of the Aconcagua team, we all came back with equal parts of euphoria and confusion. The biggest questions we faced were, "What is it that really shifted?" and "What do we do with this experience now that we are back?"

Men are prone to returning to their old ways. There is a certain comfort in the status quo, and the status quo is the very place where men retreat when fear and approval blind them to the opportunities of integration.

The Rolo Denali Project

Here is an example of how the lines between euphoria and confusion often blur with respect to cultural integration.

The seven of us were sitting in our tent at High Camp One at 16,300 feet after an extraordinarily exhausting day that had seen us climb 2,000 feet higher than any of us had ever been before, including Eric. It was a rough day for some of us: headaches, nausea, altitude sickness, and fatigue. It was also one of those days when we exalted at where we were, what we were trying to accomplish, and whom we were sitting across from. We'd just eaten dinner. It wasn't Base Camp food served restaurant-style by members of our tour company, but it was plentiful and filling and no one was complaining.

Our conversation that night had an energetic edge to it and turned to the subject of post-climb possibilities.

243

What were we going to do as a team once we returned home? How could we facilitate our preparation-phase commitment to service?

There was some exploratory discussion about starting a non-profit consulting firm that would focus on helping small businesses and start-ups gain traction in the marketplace. It was a heady conversation. Here we were, seven men with a tremendous amount of experience and enough diversity to make it feasible. But it was too much, too soon.

"Let's think about something smaller and more immediate," I said. "Just one thing to get the ball rolling."

"How about helping Rolo get to Denali? He talks about it all the time," someone said. Rolo was our third guide: a young, rugged Argentine with an easy, infectious smile. It was impossible not to like him. He had climbed Aconcagua many times, but his dream was to, one day, summit Denali, the highest peak in North America, and one of the Seven Summits.

The problem, not surprisingly, was time and money. We couldn't just take a month out of our lives, leave behind wives, girlfriends, and small children, and fly to Alaska. We would incur costs for everything from airfare and hotel accommodations to expeditionary fees and specialized equipment. It would likely take a $15,000 investment.

"Let's make it happen for him," someone else said. The excitement level about the idea amazed me. Everyone jumped on board.

**Imagine helping one young man
realize a lifelong dream.**

And as our discussion progressed, it seemed immensely doable. Greg could use his contacts in the hotel industry to provide hotel accommodations. We could all pitch in for Rolo's airfare. We could arrange a fundraiser to defer some of the other expenses. Our tent had all the energy of a brainstorming session for a fledging start-up. We went so far as to set a date for his trip: May 2012. We even gave the idea a name: The Rolo Denali Project. It had a good ring to it.

"We need someone to head up the project," I said. "Any volunteers?"

Troy raised his hand. "I'll do it," he said. "I'll put it together."

Here was an opportunity for Troy to demonstrate his leadership skills and to take ownership of something special.

The Rolo Denali Project had just been grist for a good conversation not an hour before; suddenly it was starting to sound like a reality. I wanted to make sure everyone was on the same page, because this could represent the Aconcagua Man Project starting down the road of service that we had promised each other during the preparation stage of the project.

"You're saying you'll coordinate putting the trip together with all the necessary accommodations," I fed back to Troy, because it was a big responsibility. Perfect for the integration phase once we were home. "Is that accurate?"

"Definitely," he said.

"And everyone else here is committed to doing his part in making it happen?" I asked, looking around the tent. "We're all on board?"

The answer was a resounding yes, and there was no doubt that everyone meant it at the time.

Coming home and making it happen, however, proved to be a different story. We got home, the day-to-day grind of making a living and renewing relationships took over, and the Rolo Denali Project was put on the backburner. It wasn't totally forgotten, but it was a long way from happening.

The point is that talking about service is easier said than done.

Cultural integration comes in many forms. There are always adjustments to be made once an "Aconcagua" endeavor has come to fruition. Reality sets in. There is the inevitable letdown.

Life in America—with the alarm ringing at five-thirty in the morning, the baby crying, and a client waiting for your complete attention—is different than life in a tent on the slopes of Aconcagua. Back there, you're in the moment, and the thought of helping Rolo fulfill his dream was easy to focus on in that moment.

We are at this writing six months out from our climb, but no one on our team has acted upon the Rolo Denali Project yet, and there are lessons to be learned here about cultural integration. First and foremost among them is that becoming the man you really want to be is easier said than done.

In today's world, men have built up a lot of baggage along the way.

I have stated without apology that I think men have become soft.

I have stated that too many men are embracing a "metrosexual" way of living that crushes the healthy polarity between the genders. No, there might not be anything wrong with a man, as it is said, "being in touch with his feminine side," but not if it makes you cautious or hesitant about getting out in the world and living your purpose. If your personal "Aconcagua" takes you on sabbatical to India for a month-long stay at the Tureya Ashram in southern India, and you return with a newfound commitment to a vegetarian diet, you've experienced cultural integration.

Let's say you traveled to New Orleans to help that city recover from the affect of Hurricane Katrina. When you returned home, you decided to sell your business of twenty years and form a foundation dedicated to educating kids about global warming. This is a true embrace of cultural integration.

After coming home from our climb, I decided to get more involved in assisting with political leadership. This is cultural integration.

An even more interesting example of this, one that I imagine the rest of the team also experienced in some way or another, is that the world seems smaller to me. It's like a young boy who goes to a major league baseball game for the first time, and everything about the experience is huge and surreal. When the same boy goes back as a grown man, he's more concerned about the pitcher's fastball or the manager's strategy. His world has gotten smaller.

For me, it seems as if I changed, while the world I left for sixteen days stayed more or less the same.

247

When I say that the world seems smaller to me, I mean that its intricacies are more important. I'm not as impressionable. I have more focus and vision. This is cultural and it's all positive.

You can bet that any service-oriented activity that stems from an "Aconcagua" enterprise embraces this cultural shift that we're discussing, but any change in a man's world-view also fits the definition.

Vince Ruland returned from our climb with a commitment to work more closely with his company's community service projects. He also saw an opportunity there to involve his daughters in more community-based activities, and he will tell you that what he experienced in South America was instrumental in this shift. This was a very poignant example of cultural integration.

Troy returned from our climb seeking a relationship healthier than the marriage he had left a year earlier. His marriage, by his own admission, had reinforced Troy's lifelong need for approval from the women in his life. During the preparation phase of the climb, he was honest with our team about his need to break away from that sort of emasculating behavior and he was determined to do so. And yet, he fell into the very same sort of relationship upon our return from Argentina. The relationship began to swallow him up. The good news is that Troy recognized the pattern early on and made a change; earlier in the book, you read his letter apologizing to the team about pulling away from us, but really, no apology was necessary. Troy was working the integration phase of the Aconcagua Man Project in his own way and taking responsibility for it. He is a good and loving man and I know he will discover this part of this Aconcagua experience.

Cultural integration is a strong force. It can also be an uncomfortable force. Together, these two, seemingly divergent, forces add up to continuing opportunities to grow and change. A man who embraces those opportunities with self-honesty is living deeper in his integrity.

And what is a man living with self-honesty and integrity but a man inching closer to his purpose?

21 SPECIFIC INTEGRATION

The second, but equally undeniable, type of integration that every "Aconcagua" enterprise reaps is what I call specific integration.

Specific integration is represented by concrete and definable changes that will come along with every major undertaking that pushes a man out of his comfort zone.

It is as irrefutable as it is undeniable. A man cannot experience something that makes him feel uncomfortable —like so many things will do if we commit ourselves to the search for the men we truly want to be—without spurring some degree of growth and change. That is the beautiful thing about reaching out for your purpose in life; you have to push yourself into the realm of the uncomfortable.

―――

Specific integration, unlike cultural integration, is marked by very specific action.

―――

Greg came home from the climb and committed himself to traveling less for his job and putting more focus on his family. He accomplished the first by abdicating his sales position with IHG—a very lucrative position, it should be mentioned—and accepting a promotion as a cultural leader with the firm. He is also exploring a most significant career change as a sales consultant.

Eric came off the mountain knowing he had to do something different than what he'd been doing before we left for Argentina, including an even more life-changing career move than Greg's. From mountain guide to mortgage broker is a big-time switch. Interesting, the climb shook Eric to his core. Summiting Aconcagua fulfilled an ache deep inside. It served as a release, as the accomplishment of what was really an unspoken goal. Along the way, it seeded the desire for a family. I remember the look in his eye as we descended. It was clarity of purpose. Eric and Adina are now the proud parents of Sebastian Wolf Wiseman. Adina actually became pregnant during the first month of his return from the mountain. Serendipity? Miraculous? You decide.

These are two very dramatic, if not uncommon, examples of specific integration. It is virtually impossible to take significant action without causing another action to occur, particularly when there is discomfort or unfamiliarity attached to the first action. Think about your own life. Think about your last "Aconcagua." Yes, I mean the last thing that pushed your boundaries or knocked you off center. Was it a job switch or an unprecedented adventure? Was it a change in a significant relationship or the commitment to a new hobby? Was it a move? Was it a conscious change in your lifestyle?

**Whatever it was, you're different,
so you look at life differently.
It is inevitable. It is irrefutable.**

Yes, Jeff might very well have proposed to his girlfriend at some point in the future, but he will be the first to admit that the Aconcagua climb pushed him forward; he knew that he wanted that commitment before he was even off the mountain. And yes, he may have changed his business model at some point down the road, but the climb shifted his thinking and allowed him to be more selective in his clientele.

The key is specific commitments to what has been integrated.

As men, we have to stop shying away from things that make us feel less than confident. As men, we have to stop shying away from those internal urges that are really at the heart of our dreams.

I set the stage for this feeling of "discomfort" with a set of questions that prefaced the Aconcagua Man Project invitation that I sent out to nearly a hundred men. Here's a sampling:

How does your relationship with the woman in your life impact your deepest purpose? What if you could find your physical edge again? How would that be good for your life?

How would your life be enhanced if you had discipline over food, alcohol, and sex? Are you sitting on the couch more than you know you should?

What is the one thing you must accomplish before you die, to feel you have really lived? How would living edgy assist your financial gain?

These are not questions for the squeamish, but I was not trying to pull punches. I was trying to initiate some hard thinking. If a man felt uncomfortable pondering these questions, so much the better.

And maybe key among those questions was the one surrounding purpose.

Do you really feel like you're doing what you're supposed to be doing on this earth?

Training hard for nine months in preparation for our climb was physically uncomfortable. We have talked about that. It also set the stage for frank and uncomfortable conversation about who the seven of us were as men, if we really had a clue about our purpose, and if we did, were we really fulfilling it.

Dennis, at sixty-seven, came right out and admitted where he stood on this when he said to us one day, "I haven't even begun to do what I came here to do." Admitting that you're sixty-seven and still searching takes courage, especially for a man who has accomplished as much as Dennis has.

It took Greg's astute stepfather to remind him, some days before our climb, about his true purpose when he said, "Greg, your 'Aconcagua' isn't a mountain in Argentina. Your 'Aconcagua' is right here. It's your family."

What sixteen uncomfortable days on the slopes of the real Aconcagua did was shine a very harsh and introspective light on the subject of truth and understanding.

Coming off the climb was, in many ways, a moment of truth. Did we embrace the specific and cultural integration phases once we'd returned to our day-to-day lives? That was a question that couldn't be ignored.

Here is one hard fact. No man can pursue an "Aconcagua" endeavor without facing the illumination of integration. You can ignore it, but that would be foolish, if not impossible. The change and growth of climbing your personal Aconcagua is the primary reason for the quest.

Dennis's challenge was the same as Greg's. It's the same as it was for Jeff, Vince, Troy, Eric, or me. First, embrace the shift. Secondly, let the shift wash over you. And finally, act on it.

The "taking action" part of this equation is the most important. There has to be a consequence, if you will, to any serious enterprise that a man entertains.

Action is always the sole determinant of performance on any level.

For example, a man who committed himself to a mainly whole plant food diet and a daily exercise program over the course of a month might lose fifteen pounds; we'd call this his personal "Aconcagua," and it would be completely legitimate. But it is the integration phase that comes after this successful month-long-endeavor when growth and change are really consolidated. If he goes back to his old ways, it's all for nothing. If his month-long regiment evolves into a conscious change of lifestyle that is balanced and meaningful, then he is coming from a place of self-honesty. This new and improved lifestyle could even be looked at as another "Aconcagua" endeavor in the making.

The Ripple Effect

Integration is an ongoing process, especially when you've embarked on something as significant as the Aconcagua Man Project. The ripple effect of the preparation and climb can have an incredibly long life span.

There is an unconscious effect that is inevitable when a man accomplishes something significant. His confidence soars. He holds himself a little straighter. He treats people with a sense of respect and humility. And he's more excited about the next test in his life.

There is also the more conscious, deliberate effect. A man decides to get more involved in his civic responsibilities. He decides to expand his business. He decides to take two days out of every month to indulge in his love of camping. The list is different for every man, but you understand my meaning.

**The ripple effect of the integration phase can last a
lifetime, but a man has to throw the first
stone into the water.**

This ripple effect can have unusual consequences. It's not predictable. Previous to the Aconcagua Man Project, and for many years before that, I was always ready to jump at any volunteer project someone threw my way. I rarely said no to putting on a seminar or plunging into fundraising activities. People would call, and I would say yes almost without thinking. It became habitual, and service tends to lose its value as soon as it turns from a commitment to a habit.

That has all changed since returning from the climb. All of a sudden, I am saying no to all such inquiries. And not because many of them are not good causes; many are. But many have a small return in their influence on the community and even less on society.

**I knew there was something more for me.
A different focus.
A different place for my time, energy, and talents.**

When a local councilwoman issued an invitation to me to lead a task force of new and up-and-coming political and business leaders in the metropolitan Denver area, I felt the tug of cultural integration. I saw an opportunity to influence the shift and shape of the city's entire economic

257

landscape and I knew this was the kind of opportunity I wanted to get involved in. When Bill Roth, the CEO of Mount Saint Vincent Home, asked me to participate in his ambassadors program, which indirectly helps educate and care for underprivileged kids, I said yes. (See www.msvhome.org) Here were opportunities to take my vision of leadership and introduce it into working models filled with exceptional challenges. Here was a chance, as I approached my forty-ninth year, to really expand upon the leadership tools that I use every day with my clients.

I mentioned earlier how the world seemed smaller to me upon my return from Argentina, and this was a palpable example.

I said yes to those invitations.

Specific integration is about a man's willingness to say yes to the things he truly values and no to those things he does not. We can take that a step further and make this statement: specific integration is about saying yes or no without worrying about offending anyone; it's about saying yes or no without seeking the approval of others.

This "stepping forward" is significant for any man entering the integration phase of his "Aconcagua." A very large part of this is acknowledging the skills and talents that each of us has. It's about giving these skills and talents their just due and making them available to as large an audience as possible.

**Integration is not about humility.
A man owes it to himself, his family,
and the world to be bold and beautiful.**

This is not hubris or arrogance we're talking about here. This is about putting your stamp on the world. This is about knowing that the world can benefit from your talents and skills and not being shy about it.

How Do I Top This?

This question cannot be ignored.

It hits every man who reaches out for something big and actually grabs hold of it. When you go big, you have to know that there can be a letdown on the other side of it. Asking, "How do I top this?" hit every member of the Aconcagua Man Project. We had been chasing that dream for nearly a year: training, preparing, doing.

There is always a payoff for achieving, of course, but achieving on one level cannot preclude achieving on another. A letdown in the integration phase is not a failure, but it can feel like it, if you're not prepared for it.

You've seen it often. We talked about winning the Super Bowl. In the aftermath, a football player might very easily see that as the most important moment in his life, and everything after that would be downhill. That is integration in reverse. A man who wins the Super Bowl has to understand that his life might not be headline news going forward, but his life can have even more meaning because of his achievement.

Climbing Aconcagua was not totally dissimilar. The high that went into achieving the summit was powerful stuff. We had thousands of people following our progress on the Internet. We had the dreams of hundreds of people riding on our shoulders. It was an awesome feeling.

Integration after the fact is a huge challenge. A man can say, "Well, that's the best I'll ever do." Or, a man could say, "What's next? Bring it on." No, it doesn't have to be a

259

Super Bowl or a 23,000-foot-high mountain. The key to successful integration is using the achievement and the enterprise to drive you onto bigger and better things. The letdown makes this difficult.

―――――

It is almost as if life is trying to suck you back into what you used to be: back to the man you were before you committed yourself to your "Aconcagua" endeavor.

―――――

Society is a big part of this. Mediocrity and the status quo are two seemingly acceptable approaches to life. And yet, mediocrity and the status quo are the enemies of a man committed to being the best he can be, a man dedicated to living deep in self-honesty and honoring his personal integrity.

Certain members of our Aconcagua team also suffered another interesting dynamic when we returned home. I would call it a pronounced, if unintentional, distance or disconnect from the rest of the team members. This may be natural to an extent, given the time we'd spent as a team training and climbing. On the other hand, a viable part of the Aconcagua Man Project from the beginning was a commitment to the post-climb phase, in terms of service to the community and service to ourselves as men. We were committed to this as individuals, but we were also committed as a team.

The more people involved in your post-climb world, the more advantageous it is to work on specific integration. The involvement of others keeps you on task.

It heightens the feeling of responsibility. And sometimes we need that to keep moving forward.

Isolation doesn't serve integration. Isolation makes it easier to be sucked back into the life we had before our "Aconcagua" endeavor. That is the last thing any of us on the Aconcagua team wanted.

The beauty of time passing after returning from Argentina in February was that the disconnect, the distance, and even a sense of depression lifted. The positive residual of the climb may have been cloaked for a time—and this can happen in the aftermath of any important undertaking—but then it slowly began to surface.

What does this positive residual look like? It looks like an emerging clarity of purpose, a greater sense of integrity, a heightened love of nature, and a clearer path to self-honesty.

Gradually, a more confident man emerges, and integration begins to take its natural path.

22 SEX AND THE RITE OF PASSAGE

It would be a mistake to think that a man can only go through a rite of passage in his teenage years, crossing over into manhood via some well-defined ritual at the age of twelve or thirteen. Too often, this doesn't happen in American society in any case. We have things like confirmation or a Bar Mitzvah. In Australia, the Aboriginals have the walkabout. The ancient Greeks had the Trials of Manhood.

On the other hand, American men do not, for the most part, have a defined rite of passage. Somewhere along the line, sending a boy out into the woods to forage for himself for a week was deemed too dangerous. Somewhere along the line, it became acceptable for a boy to remain in his mother's shadow until such time as he left for college, got a job, or fell in love.

This is a sad statement. The passage from childhood to adulthood should be marked by something other than the right to vote or buy a beer. We no longer recognize our entrance into manhood. That is a powerful word that has been emasculated over the last fifty years.

"Be a man" should be a statement we're proud to say.

Instead, it's become an admonishment used when a boy doesn't know how to be a man because he's never been shown. For the most part, young men in America are coddled. They're spoiled. They're told it's okay to play it safe. They're told that everyone's a winner no matter what they do or don't do. They are acknowledged for being mediocre.

I grew up without a father during my formative years. If it hadn't been for my love of sports and the testosterone rush of competition, I shudder to think what I might have become. Sports are one place in American society where boys have the chance to be boys. If sports are not your thing, then the challenges of asserting your "maleness" are limited.

Men need a rite of passage. When Eric Wiseman came down from Aconcagua ready and willing to tackle the wonders of fatherhood, I would be willing to state without equivocation that he had experienced a rite of passage. It was a beautiful thing to see.

I am forty-nine years old, but our return from Aconcagua left me with a sense of calm and confidence that was far more pronounced than what I had before I went. I came back different and ready to take on a new set of possibilities in my life.

Greg's rite of passage took a different turn. He returned from Aconcagua realizing that it was acceptable to put family ahead of career.

That is essentially what a rite of passage is. It is the crossing of a bridge from one stage in your life to another. Men should always be in search of the next bridge and the next bridge after that, but we're rarely encouraged to do so.

———

There is no age limit to a rite of passage.

———

It's not limited to our teens, twenties, or thirties. Dennis Carruth, at sixty-seven, will very likely experience a rite of passage when he puts the real estate industry behind him for good and begins to write full time. A rite of passage is an ongoing episode in a man's life. It's not a one and done proposition. It is part of a cycle that a man creates for himself.

Does a man choose to live on the edge where, as I like to put it, things are "juicy?" Does he choose to push himself into arenas that are risky? Does he choose to push the boundaries of his comfort level to explore those dreams or aspirations that may go as far back as childhood? Does he refuse to step back from his dreams or aspirations because of a lack of money or a lack of time, the classic excuses for inaction? Does he refuse to hear "you can't do that" from the mouths of people who would just as soon see him playing by society's rules?

Or does a man choose the comfort of the status quo, a place where everyone expects him to reside because it's safe and predictable, everyone, that is, except for those people who see more in him than he sees in himself? This is the place where complacency rules. This is a place where men rely on society to dictate their next move in

265

life. It could be a job they don't want or a pill they take to revive their sex life. The opportunity for a rite of passage does not exist there.

———

That place on the edge is where you and I can experience an ever-evolving rite of passage affirming our manhood and reaffirming our personal integrity.

———

The Aconcagua Man Project used Mother Nature to propel us to our edge, but it could just as easily be another man's decision to write a book or teach part-time at the local community college.

What is it that turns you on? What is it that gets the juices flowing? What is it that makes you feel uncomfortable? Answer those three questions and you're onto something that pushes you closer to the man you want to be. It also pushes you closer to your one final question: What is your Aconcagua?

Sex and the Rite of Passage
How does a man's sex life and his quest for a life of integrity and self-honesty work together, you might ask.

For me, the answer is clear. A man who can't fuck his life wide open is not going to be able to open up his woman either. This is not a chauvinistic statement by any means. This is a statement about men and women living fully. I feel that life is meant to be lived with gusto, enthusiasm, and energy. Our lives with the women we love are meant to be lived in the same way.

There is a wonderful, healthy polarity that exists between the genders. That's the way we were created: the

266

male of our species existing in harmony with the female of our species. That polarity is filled with magnificent energy that has the full potential of bringing out the best in both genders. This is not about dominance, power, or control, not at all. This is about fulfilling our souls' natures as men and women.

Society wants us to mute that polarity, as in, "Let's be more alike." I can't think of a more debilitating idea.

The fact is, however, we have become de-polarized. If you want proof, go out onto the street and ask ten women to describe the excitement level of their relationship. Most will rate it as fair at best, and many will say there is no excitement level at all.

Deep down inside, women want their men to help them open their hearts more. They want men who are passionate about their goals and dreams and are willing to take action to make them happen. A man who is living his life wide open and going for the gusto is probably going to be making more money than the man who is playing it safe. And even if he's not, he's going to refuse to work in an environment that is sucking the life out of him. I can guarantee you that there are few women who wouldn't approve of this wholeheartedly. And those women will more than likely be far more receptive when that kind of man walks through the door at night.

Most women, when all is said and done, want their men to be living their lives wide open.

They want their men seeking something bigger and more purposeful: doing work they enjoy, living their lives

267

as leaders, coming home jazzed about their world, and discovering who they are and sharing that discovery with them. That's exciting. And that excitement, when embraced by both parties, transcends their relationship, including the sexual aspects of their relationship.

Sex with the woman you love is not a right. It's a rite of passage. It is an exploration of your relationship from all sorts of amazing angles. Every time you share yourself physically with the woman in your life, you travel to a new place inside your own manhood, both physically and emotionally; some would say spiritually. It has nothing to do with performance. It has to do with strengthening your bonds with another person and also strengthening the bonds with yourself.

Combining sex with love is a powerful rite of passage, but only if you're living your life wide open, and only if you're chasing your personal dreams with purpose and commitment.

———

When you're caught in a rut, your sexuality is affected.

———

When you don't feel good about yourself physically, you're not going to want to share yourself physically. When you feel beat down at work, sex doesn't sound that appealing, mostly because you also feel beat down as a man.

The best Viagra on the planet doesn't come in a pill. It comes from living your life wide open and making absolutely no apology for it.

Consciousness and the Opposite Sex

When I say, "Fuck your life wide open," when I refer to going after all the things you want in your life with enthusiasm and gusto, what we are talking about more than anything is "consciousness." This is an esoteric word that means, in short, being awake. It means being aware of your surroundings. It means being alive to the possibilities that surround you. It means being aware of your own existence, your own thoughts, your own emotions, and the sensations that make you feel good.

A man can't read those words without wanting that for himself. That's what living fully is all about.

Here is what we, as men, need to know. What a woman wants more than anything else is to feel she is permeated by consciousness. Women want to feel the depth of consciousness of their men. They want to feel that they are awake to the world and to them. They want to feel that their men are jazzed by their surroundings, and jazzed by them. They want men who are open to the waves of opportunity that the world is washing over them every day, and that they're riding that wave together.

Feeling that way, when all is said and done, is sexy to a woman.

It's even sexier than the act of making love itself, because it adds dimension upon dimension to the relationship. And when the depths of a man's consciousness bolster the relationship, powerful and meaningful physical sex follows instinctively.

269

What does this mean? It means get up off the couch and take the bull by the horns. You can only find the depth of your consciousness by exploring the uncomfortable, by chasing your dreams, and by saying yes to your own personal "Aconcagua."

Picture this scenario. You're sitting across from the woman in your life and she is thinking, "God, he's so inspired it makes me want him!"

This doesn't happen to men who come home from work, pop open a beer, and settle in front of the television. Sure, there is a time and place for that, but it's not every night of the week; it's not even close to every night of the week.

This happens when a man is living his life wide open. This happens when a man is living on the edge where it's "juicy." This happens when a man says yes to the Aconcagua endeavors that have been calling to him all of his life.

Unfortunately, this takes direct aim at a problem far too common for men in this day and age. They are playing it safe in their lives.

They're playing it safe in their jobs and their relationships. And playing it safe is the same as saying, "I'm going to sacrifice my hopes and dreams, because that's just the way life is." How disastrous does that sound? How completely void of "consciousness" is that? You cannot be fully awake to the possibilities of life if you're playing it safe.

How often have I heard men say, "I have to stay in this job," or "I don't have the time or money for that."

This is an important point. Too many men these days fall back on the phrase, "I have to..."

I'm here to say that you don't "have to." If you choose to, then you have entered another realm, and that is the realm of self-honesty. "I choose to support my family. I choose to stay in a job I am not completely satisfied with."

When you come from a place of "I have to," you emasculate yourself. There is no depth of consciousness there, because, as I just said, you're not willing to be alive to the possibilities surrounding you. When you come from a place of "I choose to," you empower yourself, because you're suddenly aware of your existence and all the sensations of being fully awake. Interestingly, however, you also expose yourself. Why? Because now you have placed yourself in a world with options, and options force you to act.

Some men see this as dangerous ground. Others see it as liberating.

———

When you are liberated, you are free to explore depths of consciousness that the woman in your life will immediately be drawn to.

———

The end result will be a relationship with more pop to it, more energy, and yes, more sexual satisfaction.

The Learning Side of Living Wide Open

The Aconcagua Man Project was, for all seven members of our team, a rite of passage as measured by any standard. A rite of passage, if seen as such, is a powerful high. It can be almost spooky in its intensity. And, as with all highs, there is an ebb that naturally follows the flow. It's a natural part of the integration phase of any Aconcagua endeavor.

There is a letdown after running a marathon. Your body has to rest. You may not exercise for a week or a month.

After we came off the mountain into the town of Mendoza, I spent four days drinking beer and wine and allowing my mind and body just to ratchet down from the extraordinary events of the climb. It was as if I couldn't comprehend the enlightened nature of the experience.

———

This is all part of integration. We're not meant to go full-throttle all the time.

———

In fact, the downtime is vital for synthesizing the full weight of the rite of passage we've just experienced.

Integration is more than just acting upon the "Aconcagua" experience. It's about learning from the experience. It's about learning about yourself, about the world, and about change. With every learning experience, your perception evolves. And as your perception evolves, so does your view of the world and the action you take in the world. That is what a rite of passage signifies.

272

23 MONKEY OFF THE BACK

A man goes out into the world intent on conquering something. The Aconcagua Man Project, as a prime example, set out to conquer the great and ominous "colossus of America," as the locals refer to Aconcagua.

In the classic movie *Rob Roy*, one of my favorite films, our eighteenth-century hero battles injustice and the feudal Scottish landowners of his time, seeking justice and equality for the common man.

In my hometown of Denver, a current client told me the story of how he went home one day and told his wife of his plans to leave a lucrative sales position with a well-known electronics firm with the intention of starting his own sales and marketing consulting company. No questions asked.

These are all good stories, all with their own form of adventure, potential heroism, and willingness to explore the unknown. But here's the truth of the matter. None of these stories are really about a man or group of men setting out to conquer something external in the world. As any man in pursuit of something in the external world, each of these men was going out to conquer, in fact, something deep inside himself: inner truth, self-honesty, personal integrity.

———

**It is this "something" that allows a man
to navigate a depth of consciousness inwardly
and then apply it into the world.**

———

This simple statement is the sum total of the integration of any endeavor. A man who first looks at himself with self-honesty is then primed to direct his influence and his energy toward his family, his career, and the community, and to do so in complete alignment with personal integrity.

What is this depth of consciousness? It is a calm confidence. It is a comfort level with yourself. It is clarity of purpose. It is knowing that you're moving closer to the man you want to be. It is also the recognition that growth and change in a man is perpetual. It is also understanding that your growth and change are contingent upon pushing the boundaries; that your evolution is tied to that wonderful sense of discomfort that tells you that you're not stagnant, not complacent, and not willing to accept the status quo.

Now take that sense of heart, mind, and soul and put it out into the world for all to see and from which all can benefit, remembering that a depth of consciousness is as immovable as it is unshakable.

———

Integration without sharing is incomplete. We share our gifts and we share our struggles. We share our accomplishments and we share our failings. We share our love of life.

———

Saying No

A woman I fully trust came to me several months after my return from Aconcagua with an exceptional business deal. It required an investment of time and money on my part, but the upside was significant. While I won't go into the details, it was, in many ways, and by most people's estimation, a "no-brainer."

I said, "No, thank you. I appreciate it. But no."

My friend more or less said, "Are you crazy? Why would you say no?"

And my reply was, "Because that's not where I'm going with my life and my career. I know where I'm going, and that's not it."

For me, this was a full expression of the depth of consciousness that came out of the Aconcagua Man Project. I could have taken her offer, but it would have been a betrayal of my integrity. Here was an opportunity for unabridged self-honesty, and very little in this life feels better than being completely honest with yourself.

———

Self-honesty and truth are not only about saying no when it's appropriate, but men in this day and age have a very difficult time saying that word.

———

We have to get better at it. "No, that's not right for me." "No, I can do better." "No, I'm not looking for your approval."

On the flip side, we also have to be willing to say yes when it honors our integrity. We have to be willing to say yes when the opportunity for growth and change is staring us in the face. "Yes, I'm doing this thing because I'll be a better man for it." "Yes, I'm doing this thing, even without your approval, because my heart and soul tell me it's right for me." "Yes, I've found my Aconcagua, and I intend to pursue it."

Saying yes is no more selfish than saying no. These are words we have to be comfortable with using when the opportunity to become better men avails itself. Everyone in our world benefits: family, friends, colleagues, and members of our community.

As men, we cannot be afraid to pose this most imperative question: "How can I change the world? What small or big thing can I do to influence one person or a million? And, as men, we cannot be fearful of failing, fearful of being disapproved, or fearful of rejection. We have to be willing to say without equivocation, "I'm going to do this thing anyway. I'm going to do it with the power of my conviction. I'm going to do it the very best I can, because that's who I am."

Think of it as a mantra, "I'm going to do it anyway."

The Authentic You
The world is a mess. Most of us would agree on that. But you cannot avoid the mess, because the only way to have any influence on righting the ship of the world's current dilemmas is to go deeper into the mess: to throw yourself in feet first and to get involved; to embrace the

276

fact that you're going to get dirty, and to know that the mess is dying for your leadership. As a great man once told me, "Learn to love the mess."

———

This is part of integration. It is the heart and soul of both cultural and specific integration.

———

For too many years, I avoided the mess. I was too good for the mess. I didn't want to be dragged down. For too many years, I would do anything to appease someone else at the expense of the authentic me; it happened in business and it happened in my personal life. It was only when I realized that I was part of the mess, and that I loved myself for the mess that I was, that I was able to be a true leader.

You need to jump feet first into the mess to discover the authentic you. It's about really being the authentic you, once you've made that discovery. You do that not by standing aloof from the mess. You do that by believing in your gifts as a man and a human being and trading on them in the world.

———

This begins when we as men stop trying to "be something" in the eyes of society. This begins when we stop trying to live up to someone else's expectations.

———

Know what you want and go after it. We've all had our moments of greatness; now we want to find consistency in those moments.

I once had a friend describe a typical man's existence in the most poignant way. He said, "For most guys it's hassle, hassle, hassle, victory. Hassle, hassle, hassle, victory." We need to flip this around and set our sights on something more fruitful, such as, "Victory, victory, victory, and a little hassle." We need more victory and less hassle.

A step in the right direction is being true to yourself with complete and total self-honesty, and then sharing it. Don't be stingy with your gifts. Get them out into the world. You'll be amazed at the impact you'll have.

A Created World Moving Forward

Your life in the integration stage of an Aconcagua endeavor is a "created world" moving forward. This applies to your personal life; stagnation is not your friend in any relationship.

It applies to the workplace; the new leaders in the business world will be the ones who create a space that people "live into."

It applies to the community; you will become a vehicle for change and progress because you will no longer accept mediocrity.

――――

A "created world moving forward" is a by-product of a man's search for his true self and the depth of consciousness we've been discussing.

――――

Be assured that the process of discovering this depth of consciousness is an ongoing process. But once you've touched the plane of self-honesty and inner truth, you'll experience integration at its most compelling level.

278

And the most compelling discovery of all, when you've plumbed the depths of consciousness, is that you come away from it with the assurance that you no longer have anything to prove. You are a man comfortable enough with yourself to know that who you are and what you're intent upon achieving is contingent upon no one's approval, no one's praise, and no one's celebration.

Getting the monkey off your back is not an indictment of approval, praise, or celebration, not at all. Having nothing left to prove means that you are the captain of your own ship. The direction you choose to steer cannot be misguided, because it is based in self-honesty and clarity of purpose. It is also based on the fact that you will always have more to learn about yourself.

You will always have new horizons to explore.

You will always have another "Aconcagua" to carry you closer and closer to being the man that you aspire to be.

And most importantly, you will always have the drive to do what it takes to become that man.

ACONCAGUA EQUIPMENT LIST

FEET

- ≅ Socks - 3 pair outer socks, thick synthetic or wool, 3 pair inner socks, thin silk or synthetic, 1 pair Vapor Barrier Liner (VBL) socks (optional), 2 pair cotton socks (for approach hike)
- ≅ Plastic double mountaineering boots for above Base Camp, NOT SINGLE BOOTS
- ≅ Lightweight hiking boots or sturdy approach shoes for hike to Base Camp
- ≅ Booties, down or polar guard, with cordura soles (for around camp and in tent, above Base Camp)
- ≅ Gaitors (for scree, Gore-Tex type work well - NOT over-boots)
- ≅ One pair of the following for river crossings: neoprene booties with sole, Velcro-strapped rubber sole sandals (such as Tevas or Chacos), or old tennis/running shoes
- ≅ Lightweight running shoes for hike out on last day, (and for river crossings on approach hike)

UPPER BODY

- ≅ Lightweight synthetic turtleneck - 2
- ≅ Expedition weight synthetic shirt - 1
- ≅ Heavy fleece jacket
- ≅ Breathable windproof outer jacket, such as Gore-Tex, with hood

- ≅ Heavy weight down or polar guard expedition parka with insulated hood (-20 oF)
- ≅ Cotton T-shirts - 2
- ≅ Lightweight, breathable, long sleeved shirt for sun-protection on approach hike

LOWER BODY
- ≅ Synthetic or nylon briefs or underpants - 3 pair
- ≅ Lightweight synthetic or capilene long underwear bottoms - 1 pair
- ≅ Expedition weight synthetic or capilene long underwear bottoms - 1 pair
- ≅ Fleece pants (full length side zippers recommended)
- ≅ Breathable windproof pants or bibs such as Gore-Tex (full length side zippers recommended)
- ≅ Shorts - 1 pair for approach hike
- ≅ Lightweight cotton or synthetic breathable pants for sun protection - for approach hike/Base Camp

HANDS
- ≅ Mitts, fleece, or wool Dachstein - 2 pair (to fit inside one another with finger room)
- ≅ Gore-Tex wind shells for mitts - 1 pair
- ≅ Gloves, polypropylene or capilene - 1 pair for lower mountain
- ≅ Insulated, windproof, fingered gloves, such as ski gloves – 1 pair, for upper mountain
- ≅ Insulated overmitts for summit day - 1 pair

HEAD
- ≅ Ski hat, wool or fleece
- ≅ Balaclava, wool, fleece or capilene

≅ Baseball cap

SLEEPING GEAR
≅ Down or polarguard sleeping bag rated to -20 °F
≅ 1 closed cell foam pad or 1 inflatable Thermarest pad (full length). BOTH recommended.

PACK
≅ Pack, 6000 cubic inch capacity
≅ Day and a half pack for approach (approx 2000 - 3000 cubic inch capacity)
≅ Extra-large strong duffel bag WITH LOCK (about 7000 cubic inches/140 liter). THIS IS YOUR MULE BAG. Must be able to fit full expedition pack & double boots in this bag for mule to carry on approach.
≅ 1 compression stuff sack with straps - to use as a daypack for hike out on last day

TECHNICAL EQUIPMENT
≅ Ice axe 70 cm. approx. Standing with your arm relaxed at your side, ice axe should reach from the palm of your hand to the ground. For Polish Glacier Route it can be 5-10 cm shorter
≅ Crampons, 12 points non-rigid recommended. For Polish Glacier Route, rigid OK
≅ Ski poles - adjustable preferred

For Polish Glacier Route only:
≅ Climbing harness, to fit comfortably over bulky clothing
≅ Carabineers, 6 regular, 2 locking
≅ 1 Ascender

283

- ≅ 30 feet of 6mm perlon rope (for rigging your ice axe, ascender and harness)
- ≅ Shorter ice axe - 60 to 65 cm
- ≅ Climbing helmet

NOTE: ICE AXE AND CRAMPONS ARE NEEDED FOR ALL ROUTES ON SUMMIT DAY.

ESSENTIAL PERSONAL ITEMS
- ≅ Head lamp and extra batteries
- ≅ Sun glasses - two pair (one as a spare)
- ≅ Ski goggles
- ≅ Sun screen lotion SPF 30 or higher
- ≅ Sun screen lip protection - 1 stick
- ≅ Skin moisturizer - 3 oz.
- ≅ Personal supply of mole skin, Band-Aids, tape, second skin, throat lozenges
- ≅ Pocket knife
- ≅ Non-breakable plastic bowl, LARGE insulated cup w/ lid, durable spoon - **NOT PROVIDED**
- ≅ 2 water bottles -1 quart capacity, wide-mouth (hard plastic) w/water bottle insulator
- ≅ Toothbrush and toothpaste
- ≅ Toilet paper - 1 or 2 rolls, in a plastic bag (such as a Ziploc bag)
- ≅ Antibiotics - 1 cycle broad spectrum (for wound or respiratory infections)
- ≅ Aspirin or Ibuprofen - 30
- ≅ Disposable lighter (always handy on a mountaineering expedition!)
- ≅ Stuff sacks 2-3, assorted sizes (also bring a compression sack to use as daypack on hike out)

284

- ≅ Iodine or similar water purification tablets – 2 to 3 new small bottles
- ≅ $300 to $400 USD cash ($1 to $10 bills) for extra meals, drinks, tips, emergencies, (larger amount if paying porters in cash)

OPTIONAL (some of these items may be left in Base Camp):

- ≅ Camera, batteries, small solar charger
- ≅ Journal, pen/pencil, book, games, i-pod
- ≅ Small towel and soap, baby wipes, foot powder
- ≅ Cotton bandana for sun protection, neck gaitor for warmth
- ≅ Pee bottle -1 qt. capacity, wide mouth, plastic Nalgene bottle with lid (highly recommended for upper mountain, label w/permanent marker)
- ≅ 1 lightweight, <u>non-glass,</u> mini thermos, 1-quart capacity, (light wt metal, highly recommended)
- ≅ 2 lbs. of your favorite lunch treat or energy bars
- ≅ Hydrating system, 2-quart capacity (i.e. camel bags) Do not count on this as a replacement for water bottles, <u>CAMEL BAGS FREEZE higher on the mountain</u>. Excellent for approach hike to Base Camp.
- ≅ Portable water purification system (be prepared to share this item with your team).

WORDS FROM THE SIX MEN

"I recall the first thought I had when "justifying" why I should even spend the time on the Aconcagua Man Project..."What could I achieve if I really pushed myself?" Even by the question I was still thinking results, production, better than before.

The project, the mountain, the team all helped to open my heart, my mind and my soul to see and feel what was truly important to me. And for the first time in my successful, results orientated life it was family... my family... my Aconcagua. I ask many in passing and in spirit, "What is your Aconcagua?" I had asked myself before leaving for Argentina, but I thought I knew. Now I am sure."

Greg Aden, VP - Franchise Sales & Development,
IHG - InterContinental Hotels Group

"For me, the Aconcagua Man Project came out of the blue, like a freight train on a collision course with my life. Unlike most of the team, I had very little time to train and prepare for the climb, I made a quick, almost rash decision to lean in to this project and then I had to break down numerous barriers to make it happen. The mountain was a chance to step out of my day to day routine and really reflect on my life, where I had been, where I wanted to go, and I had realizations about how and where I had the power to make decisions that would shape that journey. Some of those decisions were made right there on the mountain, some of them would come later, with amazing results."

Vince Ruland, Sr. Team Lead - Raytheon

"The Aconcagua Man Project was a real life changer for me....and I don't say that lightly. Putting a large, adventurous goal like Aconcagua on the horizon of my life brought about new challenges and questions about what was true for me....in all aspects of my life. I had to push myself to new levels mentally, physically, and spiritually.... After reaching the summit of Aconcagua and returning home, I had a new space from which I was able to create. A few months after the climb I started a successful new career, my wife is pregnant, and am living a more fulfilled and in touch life. I am grateful for the pain, sweat, struggles and ultimately the success that came with this project. I truly am a different man."

Eric Wiseman, Mortgage Broker

"The Aconcagua Man Project is one of the single most powerful experiences of my life. Stephen's coaching along with the incredible challenge of summiting Aconcagua created an atmosphere that had me unleashing greatness in places where I previously settled for "good." When I joined the program, I was concerned that my business might suffer due to the new time commitments. Quite the opposite, I had major increase in both my professional effectiveness as well as my income. It was so much fun to be a part of a team again and push myself and my team mates. I got in the best shape of my life and my wife loves it. This program helped me grow mentally, emotionally, physically and Spiritually. Every man deserves an experience like this."

Jeff Patterson, Coach & Speaker

"I feel that it was a great privilege and honor to have guided the Aconcagua Man Project. From the moment I met the team I knew this was going to be an expedition of a different caliber. This was a team that was physically and mentally prepared like no other. They did not come just to conquer and check another mountain off their list. They came for more and we all walked away with something greater. It allowed me to guide in a style that I always wanted to on a big mountain. I am truly grateful to have been a member of this incredible journey."

Mike Bradley, Guide

"I will never forget the morning...when you shared your vision to assemble a group of men to seek a high summit in their lives. I said "I'm a lot older than the guys you are considering, but if I join you, I will not hold you back". Real estate had been my sole and focused career for 35 years...[It]had run its course on stimulating my vision of expanding horizons and making a true difference in the world. I needed, wanted, had to make a change. So, I said yes. Yes to you, yes to an incredible group of men, yes to moving beyond my comfort zone to seek high summits and beyond. The Aconcagua journey, which saw five of our team summit with two incredible guides, is a constantly moving and evolving force in my life and in my interactions with others...I have moved aggressively into a new technology career with all its challenges and have greater clarity in my desire to mentor others toward pursuing their passions and discovering their "Aconcaguas". "

Dennis Carruth, President, Carruth Properties Co.

ABOUT THE AUTHOR

Stephen McGhee is a top business leadership consultant, author, speaker, and documentary filmmaker. For the past eighteen years, he has been leading senior level executives to go beyond self-imposed limitations to create astonishing results. His work brings extraordinary outcomes to seemingly unsolvable scenarios.

Stephen works with CEOs, CFOs, politicians, government agencies, celebrities, and world-class athletes to help them realize their potential and live the life of their dreams. He has coached the top of the house in companies like Microsoft and Kaiser and presented hundreds of keynotes both nationally and internationally.

With an undergraduate degree in finance and a Masters degree in spiritual psychology, Stephen blends a practical, result-driven mindset with an open communication style that allows him to get to the core of any situation. He calls out brilliance in leaders so they are able to inspire their teams to achieve superb, transformational results.

Stephen has led executive wilderness trips to Argentina, Chile, Idaho, and Colorado. He consistently guides individuals and groups through internal and external barriers to greater effectiveness, satisfaction, and happiness as people and as leaders.

In 2010, Stephen created The Aconcagua Man Project, a twelve-month leadership program that culminated in a climb to the summit of Aconcagua, the highest mountain outside of Asia. His documentary film chronicling the results of the inaugural program is due to be released in 2012. He is also the author of *Learning to Believe the Unbelievable: Living Life as a Miracle Leader* and his next book, titled *Get Real: Turning Possibilities into Realities*, will be available in 2012.

You can connect with Stephen on twitter, username @stephenmcghee, and follow his blog at www.McGheeLeadership.com.

Learn more about the Aconcagua Man Project at www.AconcaguaMan.com and get the latest project updates by following us on Facebook and Twitter, as below, respectively:
www.facebook.com/AconcaguaManProject
@aconcaguaman

To order additional copies of this and other books by
Stephen McGhee, visit www.McGheeLeadership.com/books.
292

Made in the USA
San Bernardino, CA
25 March 2014